COMMANDER X'S GUIDE TO INCREDIBLE CONSPIRACIES

Edited by Commander X

Global Communications

Conspiracy Journal Presents
Commander X's
Guide to Incredible Conspiracies

Timothy Green Beckley: Editorial Director
Carol Rodriguez: Publishers Assistant
Cover Art: Tim R. Swartz

For free catalog write:
Global Communications
P.O. Box 753
New Brunswick, NJ 08903

Free Subscription to Conspiracy Journal E-Mail Newsletter
www.conspiracyjournal.com

Contact Rights Manager at above address
For reprints and translations

Commander X's Guide to Incredible Conspiracies

INCREDIBLE CONSPIRACIES

UNDERGROUND BASES AND INNER EARTH MYSTERIES

PLANET X AND OTHER STRANGE EVENTS

ANOMALOUS BEINGS, REPTILIANS AND SHAPE SHIFTERS

EARTH AND CLIMATE CHANGES

SECRET SOCIETIES AND THE NEW WORLD ORDER

SUPPRESSED TESLA AND OTHER INCREDIBLE TECHNOLOGIES

Commander X's Guide to Incredible Conspiracies

INTRODUCTION
By Commander X

As I was making the final preparations for my first broadband internet lecture, an acquaintance, whom I had been trying to convince that he needed to attend my lecture, said to me: "How can you believe in all of this conspiracy crap? Everyone knows that there are no such things as conspiracies".

I know that I shouldn't have been surprised by this man's blanket dismissal of all conspiracies; after all, conspiracy theories have always been attacked as part of the "lunatic fringe". Historians have avoided dealing with conspiracy since it necessarily takes place behind the scenes. Normal sources or archives do not reveal its operators, who rarely leave a paper trail. Evidence often depends on victims who are usually not objective.

But considering that everyday the news media is reporting about one conspiracy or another, it still amazes me that many people dismiss the notion of conspiracy outright. It almost seems as if there is a conspiracy to silence conspiracy theory.

When one dares to dig beneath the surface to reveal undisclosed purposes, he or she is usually met with charges of being a "paranoid" defender of "conspiracy theories." More often than not, such an accusation silences the questioner, as it is apparently designed to do.

It's probably not surprising that any journalist or writer dealing in conspiracies winds up being accused, eventually, of trading in conspiracy theories. It kind of comes with the territory, though it used to be that in the end the results were what mattered; if you had the facts on your side, it was no longer a mere theory, but a point of substance.

Even though I don't buy into every conspiracy that is thrown at me, I gladly admit to considering any conspiracy theory for which there is credible evidence. But those who condemn me for my views never seem interested in examining the evidence, their purposes being more to prevent the raising of uncomfortable questions. I ask my critics to account for the countless foreign intrigues, plots, assassinations, alliances, and other cabals that have been at the heart of so much of the history of the world.

I would consider the operation to fly jetliners into the World Trade Center on 9/11 a conspiracy. I would consider the mailing of anthrax letters to Democratic leaders and members of the media a conspiracy. I would call the disinformation campaign targeted at the American public to justify attacking and occupying Iraq a conspiracy. And lets not forget Watergate, or the COINTELPRO episode, or the Iran-Contra scandal to demonstrate that conspiracies continue to weave their way into the fabric of American history. Yet, many still brush off notions of vast conspiracies, saying how could so many people keep a secret?

The truth is, they can't. That is where conspiracy theory comes in. This book was written because we are not being told the truth about our history. It's time for those of us who care about our future to start reclaiming our past.

I have gathered together for this book some of the best and brightest authors on the scene today to give their view on the complex world of conspiracies. It is not my intention to convince the reader of the validity of every theory presented in this book. Instead, it is up to you to decide for yourself what to believe or not to believe. Just always remember, one reason we expect conspiracies is that we have good reason to do so.

INCREDIBLE CONSPIRACIES

Conspiracies to Make Your Skin Crawl
By Brad Steiger & Sherry Hansen Steiger

Secret Government Agencies Are Creating Diseases to Depopulate the Planet

Many conspiracy theorists believe that secret agencies in governments throughout the globe are plotting to depopulate the planet by spreading diseases among the masses. Some even accuse the United Nations and its World Health Organization of utilizing viruses created in the U.S. Army's biological weapons laboratories to deliberately infect entire populations in Africa, Haiti, and elsewhere with the ghastly AIDS virus. In addition, such diseases as lassa fever, the ebola virus, and mad cow disease are all part of an insidious government program to spread biological and chemical death among the mass populations.

Other conspiracy theorists believe that another AIDs-like disease is spreading among those military personnel who served in the Persian Gulf War in 1991. Reports of this new mystery illness occurring in Gulf War vets began coming in the spring of 1992. Symptoms included chronic fatigue, muscle aches, swollen and painful joints, aching teeth and gums, memory loss, and fevers.

By 1994, military officials admitted that as many as 20,000 or more of the 700,000 troops who served in that conflict were exhibiting results of a strange disease that came to be known as the Persian Gulf syndrome. Many of those afflicted blamed the experimental vaccines that had been injected into their persons with the express goal of protecting them against anthrax, nerve gas, and other biological warfare agents suspected to be used by the troops of Saddam Hussein. Others blamed the inhalation of toxic fumes from the Kuwait oil fires or unknown chemical agents.

But this new mystery disease, according to many sources, is affecting U.S. troops who were hundreds of miles away from the area in northern Iraq where chemical detection teams recorded low-level amounts of bio-warfare agents.

One Alabama veteran of the Persian Gulf conflict is said to have stated that up to two-thirds of all reserve units came back with some symptoms of the mystery illness. Many of these personnel blame Iraqi Scud missiles that were laced with chemical agents and some kind of man-made virus. And they believe that the U.S. government is covering up knowledge of the agents of bio-warfare that are causing terrible suffering among the veterans of that war.

Those attempting to crack open the government conspiracy state that the single factor common to all troops involved in the campaign is that they were all given experimental drugs and vaccines as part of the requirement to serve in the Gulf, and conspiracy theorists argue that the U.S. military has a long history of conducting covert medical experiments on its own personnel, as well as unknowing civilians.

According to these individuals, dozens of secret, planned bio-attacks were perpetrated on American cities during the 1950s and 1960s—the most notorious being a six-day bio-attack on San Francisco in which the military sprayed massive clouds of potentially harmful bacteria over the entire city. When mind-altering drugs were developed in the 1950's, these conspiracy theorists state, the military secretly gave them to enlisted men, a conscienceless act that resulted in a number of deaths that were shamelessly covered up.

Certain watchdog groups have recently charged secret government groups with conspiring to institute a policy of global population control by giving children deadly vaccines during mandatory vaccination programs. According to these investigators, these vicious vaccines have not only caused seizures, brain damage, and death, but they have also been responsible for the unprecedented rise in criminal activity and violent crimes among children. According to these theorists, the recent rash of shootings in grade schools and high schools are a direct result of the effects of injected chemicals.

Beware the Secret Government's "Zombie Chip"

Conspiracy theorists fear that by 2010, all Americans will be forced to receive a programmable biochip implant somewhere in their body. The biochip is most likely to be implanted on the back of the right or the left hand so it will be easy to scan at stores. The biochip implant will also be used as a universal type of identification card. A number will be assigned at birth and will follow that person throughout life.

While people will be informed that the biochip will be used largely for purposes of identification, the reality is that the implant will be linked to a massive super computer system that will make it possible for government agencies to maintain a surveillance of all citizens by ground sensors and satellites.

Once the surveillance system is in place, the biochips will be implemented to transform every man, woman, and child into a controlled zombie-like slave, for these devices will make it possible for sinister agencies to influence a person's brain cells and to talk directly with the individual's brain neurons. Through cybernetic biochip brain implants, people can be forced to think and to act exactly as government intelligence agencies have preprogrammed them to think and behave.

Conspiracy theorists allege that a U.S. Naval research laboratory, funded by intelligence agencies, has achieved the incredible breakthrough of uniting living brain cells with microchips. When such a chip is injected into a man's or a woman's brain, he or she instantly becomes a living vegetable and a subservient New World Order slave! And once this device is perfected, the biochip implant could easily be converted into a "Frankenstein-type weapon," permitting the Defense Department to produce an army of killer zombies.

Parents in Palto Alto, California are convinced that their teenaged son's psychological problems are the result of a biochip that was implanted into his head by a CIA agent during a tonsillectomy. The young man is constantly receiving threats and negative thoughts through a wavelength that is received by the biochip in his brain. They swear the device has shown up on X-rays, but that CIA agents destroyed the evidence.

Before his execution, convicted Oklahoma City Federal Building bomber Timothy McVeigh frequently stated that Federal agents were able to track him during the 1990s because of an electronic monitoring device that had been placed in his leg. McVeigh was not alone in his belief that the U.S. Army secretly implanted such devices in the legs of American soldiers during the Gulf War. There have also been rumors that American astronauts were implanted with electronic devices to keep check on more than just their physical well-being.

Commander X's Guide to Incredible Conspiracies

Mysterious Black Helicopters Hover over America

Since the 1980s, hundreds of men and women have reported being harassed and spied upon by mysterious unmarked black helicopters. Those who are involved in the investigation of any suspected conspiracy or if they are doing serious UFO research, many conspiracy theorists believe such people are certain to be under surveillance by a hovering black helicopter. According to "informed" individuals, the black choppers are the property of a clandestine national police force that will soon begin to wage incessant warfare against all Americans who oppose the secret government. The pilots who fly the mystery helicopters and the black uniformed agents within the craft are the minions of the secret government which has signed a document turning over control of our nation's military forces to greedy and power-hungry international bankers, the Secret Brotherhood of the Illuminati, and their various allies.

Many conspiracy researchers believe that the crews of the black helicopters are veterans of a highly classified CIA project, which involved the training and indoctrination of selected, multiple-personality assassins. These agents were not only programmed to kill, but after repeated torture and hypnotic brainwashing sessions, they were given selective "memories" of new and fictitious lives. The CIA conducted such insidious and reprehensible experiments in mind control in the 1950s and 1960s under the code name MK-ULTRA, and the assassins produced by the program were considered a kind of secret weapon against the Soviet Union.

According to the conspiracy theorists, MK-ULTRA crews aboard the black helicopters are assigned to seek out those researchers and investigators who are becoming too much of an annoyance to the secret government. If these individuals do not desist in their investigations of the international conspiracy headed by the New World Order and the Illuminati, they will be abducted and undergo experiments in biochemical research, psychosurgery, and electrical stimulation of the brain. After repeated torture and hypnotic brainwashing sessions, they will be given selective "memories" which may include intense recall of UFO sightings and abduction experiences, causing them to be discredited by any civil authorities to whom they may later report their claims of having been abducted by agents of the secret government.

The New World Order and the Invasion from Outer Space

In 1992, when President George Bush began speaking about his hope that a New World Order had been created after the conclusion of the Gulf War (1991), he quite likely included such references to a new world structure along with the colorful imagery of a "thousand points of light" in order to beef up his campaign for reelection and to defeat the challenger, Bill Clinton. However, evangelist Pat Robertson, who was also briefly a presidential candidate, passionately spoke out that the "new world order" was actually a code for a secret group of conspirators who sought to replace Christian society with a worldwide atheistic socialist dictatorship.

George Bush, Robertson and a number of conspiracy theorists charged, was a member of one of the world's most devilish and powerful secret societies: the Order of Skull and Bones. What was more; Bush was linked to the Bilderbergers and the Trilateral Commission, dangerous elitist organizations.

About the same time that President Bush's alleged secret society affiliations were being exposed, a number of fundamentalist Christian evangelists began to take their first real notice of the UFO phenomenon and saw the mysterious aerial objects as the "signs in the skies" referred to in apocalyptic literature and in the book of Revelation as heralding the advent of the Antichrist. It was a short leap for many evangelists to begin to blend accounts of UFOs with the secret societies of top U.S. government officials, politicians, corporate chairmen, international bankers, and many others who sought to bring into being the dreaded "New World Order" and the Beast of Revelation and establish him on his throne of planetary domination.

According to the proponents of this cosmic conspiracy, when President Ronald Reagan gave his famous "alien invasion" speech to the entire United Nations General Assembly in September of 1987, he had already secretly advised representatives of the 176 member nations that the leaders of their respective governments must meet the demands of the technologically superior extraterrestrials or be destroyed. In his speech to the General Assembly, Reagan said that he occasionally thought how quickly all nationalistic differences worldwide would vanish if humanity were facing an alien threat from outside this world. And then he suggested that an alien threat was already among us.

A number of conspiracy theorists stated that Reagan's speech hinted at a plan agreed to by world leaders and extraterrestrial invaders that around the year 2000 a carefully staged "alien invasion" would convince the masses of the world that a real-life alien attack from outer space was about to begin. People of all nations would believe their leaders who would tell them that the aliens were a benevolent species and that unconditional surrender to them would be for everyone's own good.

Immediately following the surrender to the aliens, the united leaders will form a One World Government, a New World Order, thus fulfilling biblical prophecies about a return to the days of Babylon. The aliens will reveal themselves as demonic entities that delight in doing Satan's work. The planet will be in torment and turmoil until Jesus returns to deal the final blow to the minions of evil.

The Murder of Princess Diana

The incredible spectacle of world-wide mass mourning over the loss of Diana, Princess of Wales, may have quieted down to a respectful viewing of her final resting place on a small island surrounded by a tranquil pond on the ancestral mansion of the Spencer family, but conspiracy theories about her death and that of her lover Dodi Al Fayed remain as numerous as ever. With an increasing number of recently released tape recordings and eye-witnesses to various episodes in the Princess of Wales final days, the allegations continue there was bloody work afoot on that tragic evening of August 31, 1997. Among the most oft-cited charges are the following:

1. Angry international arms dealers assassinated Princess Diana because of her high-profile global campaign against the use of land mines.

Those mysterious men on motorcycles who, according to some witnesses, forced the Fayed's limousine to crash, were not wild and crazy paparazzi who became tragically over-zealous in pursuit of sensational photographs, but cold and cruel hired assassins who accomplished exactly what it was that they set out to do: Provoke the driver into dangerous speeds and cause the vehicle to crash.

2. On orders from the Royal Family, British Intelligence murdered Diana. Conservative Queen Elizabeth and her consort, Prince Philip, had been terribly upset by the whole nasty business of the divorce of Prince Charles and Lady Di, and now Diana, 36, had taken up Dodi Al Fayed, 41, a Muslim playboy, the son of Harrods department store owner Mohammed Al Fayed. What was worse, after leaving her sons William and Harry with their father, Prince Charles, Diana was openly carrying on with Dodi Fayed in a romance that was meticulously covered by the world press. And as if all such tasteless goings on were not enough, it was said that Dodi had presented Diana with a diamond-studded, star-shaped ring to seal their vows of engagement and their intention to wed.

The British press frequently reported that it was quite apparent that Prince Philip, in particular, made no effort to keep his dislike of Dodi Fayed a secret. Newspapers in the United Kingdom had reported that the Royals had even discussed dire consequences with Diana if she should continue the relationship. Among those "consequences" was possible exile – even though she was the mother of the future King of England – or social ostracism from all association with the Royal Family. Certain observers of the war of nerves between the Princess of Wales and the Royal Family suggested that Diana had grown past caring what Charles and his parents thought about her or her romances or her charitable deeds. She was now in a relationship with a man who could afford to keep her in the lifestyle to which she had become accustomed.

Conspiracy theorists maintain that when rumors began to circulate that Diana might be pregnant with Dodi's child; the Royal Family had had enough and ordered her death. And, of course, a bonus that would result for Prince Charles once Diana was out of the way was that he could now have full control over his sons, continue his adulterous relationship with Camilla Parker-Bowles, and one day ascend unencumbered to the throne of England.

3. Princess Diana paid the ultimate price for dabbling in the Dark Arts.

While Prince Charles has often been characterized as a bit off-the-wall for his interests in the supernatural, the paranormal, alternative medical practices, and environmental concerns, it was also well known that Princess Diana and Sarah Ferguson, ex-wife of Prince Andrew, sought the counsel of spiritualist mediums and psychic sensitives. Some theorists have charged that they have evidence that the Princess of Wales became deeply involved with the occult and became adept at certain techniques of sorcery. Others have said that a rather large number of Diana's close friends joined her in her forays into witchcraft, astrology, magic, and the commanding of dark forces.

Some conspiracy buffs have suggested that the death of Diana and Dodi was a result of occult practices that backfired on the Princess and that curses she had directed against her enemies had somehow boomeranged and unleashed their malignant energy upon Diana and her lover. Evil and mysterious forces were at work that fatal night of August 31, 1997, and demonic forces took the life of one who too carelessly had opened a door to a dark dimension.

4. Diana was killed because she had offended a powerful secret society.

Closely related to the theory that Diana's dabbling in the dark side of the occult caused her death is the allegation that certain of her public activities had disturbed the inner circle of men who operate in secrecy behind the scenes in Great Britain, the European nations, and the United States, who fervently believe that the Royal family of England is in direct lineage of the Throne of David, the House of Jacob, and the actual blood line of Jesus. Some theorists firmly insist that this secret society did not approve of the public and private actions of Lady Di and pronounced her death sentence before she further embarrassed the Royals.

Commander X's Guide to Incredible Conspiracies

5. Princess Diana and Dodi Fayed faked their deaths and are still alive.

There are the conspiracy advocates--championed largely, no doubt, by those who fervently believe that the "King," Elvis Presley, is still alive—who argue that Diana had had it with the media, the Royal Family, and the cruel pressures of society's demands upon her private life. Somewhere in some idyllic paradise, hidden away from the prying eyes of the world, the two lovers maintain a happy existence, far from the maddening and demanding crowds.

How the Warren Commission Created the "Magic Bullet" That Killed JFK

The matter of who killed President John F. Kennedy on November 22, 1963 has never been answered to the satisfaction of large portions of the populace. Various students of the terrible events which occurred that day on Dealey Plaza in Dallas, Texas, have amassed evidence to prove a large number of possible assassins, including Kennedy's own Secret Service bodyguards, the Mafia, the CIA, or Cuban activists.

While Lee Harvey Oswald continues to be the assassin of record and is named in official documents as the lone gunmen responsible for the death of President Kennedy, conspiracy buffs have always disputed the allegation that Oswald could have acted alone or that he was the kind of marksman who could have accurately hit a moving target at a considerable distance with the bolt-action rifle allegedly in his possession. Conspiracy theorists insist that there is physical, medical, and ballistics evidence that would force any fair-minded panel of experts to conclude that one person could not have fired so many shots so quickly with a single-shot, bolt-action rifle.

In 1964, the Warren Commission, a group of government officials assigned to study the assassination, concluded that a single bullet passed through President Kennedy's body and continued on a course that also allowed it to strike Texas Governor John Connally, who, with his wife, Nellie, was riding in the open car with President and Mrs. Kennedy. According to the Warren Commission, a second shot from Oswald struck the President in the head and killed him. The Commission also concluded that there had been another bullet that had missed the presidential automobile altogether, so that made four rounds allegedly fired from Oswald's bolt-action rifle in an impossible blur of time.

Conspiracy theorists immediately dismissed the so-called "magic bullet" that the government experts stated had passed through President Kennedy and continued to plow through the back, ribs, right wrist, and left leg of Governor Connolly. From the very first days of the investigation, Governor and Mrs. Connally insisted that two bullets had struck the President and that a third and separate bullet had wounded the Governor.

On July 3, 1997, former president Gerald Ford, the last surviving member of the Warren Commission, admitted that he had assisted the "magic bullet" theory in the report on JFK's death by altering the Commission's description of the gunshot that killed him.

According to Ford, the original text said that a bullet had entered Kennedy's back at a point slightly above the shoulder and to the right of the spine. Ford changed the bullet's entrance point from Kennedy's upper back to his neck, thus making the final Commission text refer to the bullet entering "the base of the back of the neck."

Such a seemingly minor alteration would support the Warren Commission's single-assassin hypothesis which was based on the "magical" path of a single bullet that was able to pass through Kennedy's neck and somehow manage to leave another six wounds on his body before striking Texas Governor John Connally's back, ribs, right

Commander X's Guide to Incredible Conspiracies

wrist, and left leg.

Skeptics of the "magic bullet" theory and the Warren Commission's final report have always pointed to the famous Zapruder home movie of the assassination and insisted that Kennedy appears hit long before Connally, who continued to hold his hat in his hand, was struck by the remarkable bullet.

Gerald Ford was a congressman when he served on the Warren Commission, and he displayed no guilt or remorse about the fraud that he had perpetrated. In fact, he told the Associated Press, "My changes were only an attempt to be more precise. I think our judgments have stood the test of time."

A poll conducted by the University of Ohio and Scripps Howard News Service in 1997 revealed that 51 percent of the American public dismissed the "magic bullet" theory. Nearly 20 percent of those polled expressed their belief that agents of the federal government assassinated Kennedy. Another 33 percent, while not wishing to go so far as to accuse government agents of having killed the president, did contend that a conspiracy of political insiders was "somewhat likely" in the murder of JFK. Regardless of government officials expressing their confidence in the findings of the Warren Commission, investigations into the truth about John F. Kennedy's assassination are not over yet.

The Bilderbergers and the New World Order

When the approximately 120 members of the ultra-secret Bilderberg Group arrive for their annual meeting at a major resort or hotel they bring together the most powerful individuals in the world, drawn from the highest executive levels of international business, education, finance, and the media. The Group first met at the Bilderberg Hotel in the Netherlands in 1954, at an event hosted by Prince Bernard and a number of luminaries from the European branch of the Illuminati. Since then, the Bilderbergers, as they began calling themselves, have met secretly each year in a different geographical location.

When asked the purpose for the international gathering of the global elite, their spokesman, Charles Muller, said that the group would be discussing issues that affected the Western world, issues such as China, Islam, energy management, NATO, corporate governance, and the growth of certain nations. Some journalists claim to have spotted Colin Powell, Henry Kissinger, World Bank President James Wolfensohn, and David Rockefeller among the attendees. There were also a few token women of power at the meeting in 1997, such as Katharine Graham, publisher of the *Washington Post*. Certain scholars that have studied the makeup of the Bilderbergers insist that the group is controlled by the ten man Inner Circle of the Illuminati. According to their claims, this secret cabal has painstakingly prepared an agenda for the masses of humanity as the world moves inexorably toward the millennium. Such individuals as the Bilderbergers will become our masters, and the vast majority of the global population may look forward to a future existence as pawns, if not slaves, of the Illuminati.

According to certain sources that claim knowledge of the basic plan for world dominance set in motion by the Bilderbergers, the following goals are among their principal objectives:

*The United States must promptly pay its debt to the United Nations. In addition, the U.S. will be asked to contribute billions of dollars to the International Monetary Fund.

U.S. taxpayers will be bled almost dry by such expenditures.

    *The North Atlantic Treaty Organization (NATO) will be converted into a United Nations military force. U.S. troops will therefore come under the command of NATO's foreign officers.

    *"Corporate Governance" will dissolve national sovereignty and bring all of the Earth's corporations under a single global order. Local control over businesses and corporations by nations and states will be terminated. The great giants of finance will be able to disregard the laws and dictates of all governments, including those of the U.S.

    *As the 21st century dawns, a new system of fascism will emerge under the guise of free trade practices which will be guided by the Illuminati.

    *The Bilderbergers have approved the Red Chinese model of economics as the standard for the emerging European superstate and the United States. As in Red China, all dissidents will be dealt with severely and placed in work camps.

    *As soon as the program can be implemented, citizens in every nation will be issued the Universal Biometrics Identification Card.

    *A Gestapo-like police state will be established to enforce the dictates of the Illuminati's New World Order.

Fighting FEMA for the Future Freedom of the United States

In the motion picture X-Files: Fight the Future (1998), FBI agents Fox Mulder and Dana Scully find themselves battling terrorists from FEMA, the Federal Emergency Management Agency. Although the film portrays the agency as a sinister syndicate with such powers that they can even suspend the United States Constitution, representatives from FEMA claim that they are a totally benign agency that responds to floods and other disasters. However, certain watchdogs of the freedoms of U.S. citizens see FEMA as very different from their own warm and fuzzy portrayal of themselves, and they argue that the dire predictions made in the X-Files motion picture is far from baseless paranoia. Conspiracy theorists state grimly that we may well be fighting FEMA for our future.

Principal among the concerns of many serious-minded guardians of our freedom and liberties is the Executive Order signed into existence by President George Bush in 1989. This document authorized FEMA to build 43 primary camps, each of which would have the capacity of housing 35,000 to 45,000 people. There are also hundreds of secondary facilities, a number of which can accommodate 100,000 individuals. The big question remains: Have these camps been constructed in preparation for some great future cataclysm that will deprive millions of people of their homes and force them to take shelter in the barracks-style housing thoughtfully prepared for such an emergency by the benevolent FEMA? Or are these camps designed by the federal government to hold prisoners of the state? Rather than refugee camps, are they concentration camps constructed to isolate those citizens who dare to oppose a new political order in the United States?

Conspiracy theorists are concerned that there are Executive Orders that grant frightening powers to FEMA and actually permit the government agency to suspend the United States Constitution and all the rights and liberties of U.S. citizens, as those rights are now known. The watchdog groups point out that these orders are in the Federal Register located in Washington DC where they may be examined by all concerned citizens who may wish to judge for themselves the awesome potential control of FEMA over all Americans and over every aspect of American life.

Executive Order #12148 stipulates that FEMA is in charge during national security emergencies, such as national disasters, social unrest, insurrection, or a national financial crisis.

According to Executive Order #10995, FEMA may, if it deems it necessary to accomplish its goals, seize all communications media in the United States.

Executive Order #10997 provides for the seizure of all electric power, petroleum, gas, fuels, and minerals, both public and private.   Executive Order #10998 allows the seizure of all food supplies and resources, public and private--and all farms, lands, and equipments.   Executive Order #10999 provides for the seizure of all means of transportation, including personal cars, trucks, or vehicles of any kind and total control over all highways, seaports, and waterways.

Executive Order #11003 allows the government to take over all airports and aircraft--commercial, public, and private.

Executive Order #11005 provides for the seizure of all railroads, inland waterways, and public storage facilities.

Conspiracy watchdogs are greatly worried about Executive Order #11000, which allows FEMA to seize all American people for federally supervised work forces. If the government branch deems it necessary, they may even split up families. Executive Order#11004 allows the Housing and Finance Authority to relocate entire communities and to designate new areas to be abandoned and new locations to be repopulated.

All of the orders listed above--and many others--were combined by President Richard Nixon into Executive Order #11490, which permits the government to take control if the President of the United States should declare a national emergency. Conspiracy theorists state that they become very nervous when they consider all the "national emergencies" that are declared each year, and they worry that FEMA may one day decide it is time to exercise the extraordinary powers that have been granted to its agency.

Visit Brad and Sherry Steiger at their website: www.bradandsherry.com

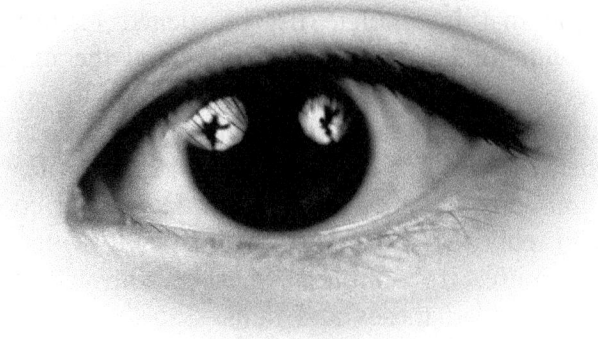

Commander X's Guide to Incredible Conspiracies

A Tale of Two Conspiracy Writers
By Kenn Thomas

That the legends of Jim Keith and Kerry Thornley live on impresses me a great deal. I knew both of these extraordinary conspiracy writers and at the time I guessed that they would spend their careers in obscurity. Both were heroes to me, of course, but fame and a broad-based impact on the world never loomed large in my expectations. The ideas of parapolitical analysts always percolate below the mainstream political world, shining some light on that latter's foundations but usually only for the minority that wants to pay attention.

Keith felt differently. He told me he aspired to become a "hip Bill Cooper". Conspiracy aficionados recognize the late Cooper (1) as someone very difficult to admire personally but an author who wrote a classic of conspiracy literature, *Behold A Pale Horse* (2). A cranky personality prevented Cooper from finessing the success of his book into anything other than cult status. Keith, however, recognized the appeal of the material and was determined to transform it with his own charm and sense of humor. By this means, he would make a writing career that would actually pay his rent.

To a certain extent he did become a hip Bill Cooper. Keith's popularity grew enormously from its roots in the zine underground, where *Dharma Combat*, *Notes from the Hangar* and other small products of his creativity and photocopier access provided a platform for many obscure writers. (4) He brought several of these writers into an anthology of commentary on the *Gemstone File*, his first real book outside of a paperback porn novel published by Masquerade that Keith wrote under a pseudonym (5). This began Keith's long association with Ron Bonds' IllumiNet Press, the same press that first published Kerry Thornley's Idle Warriors. The association with IllumiNet led to the long line of Keith books that certainly enhanced his stature with his fan base: *Casebook on Alternative 3*; *Casebook on the Men in Black*; *Mass Control: Engineering Human Consciousness*; *OKBomb! Conspiracy and Cover Up* – still the best source on the conspiracy currents of the Oklahoma City bomb; one wonders what other information Keith could have accumulated over 9/11 (6); *Biowarfare in America* (another one of great contemporary relevance following the post-9/11 anthrax scares); and the two Black Helicopter books, *Black Helicopters over America* and *End Game Strategy*.

The last two on that incomplete list broadened Keith's appeal. It gained a tremendous audience with fundamentalist Christians and the militia groups that often held up Bill Cooper as a spokesman. Keith was hip enough to work that crowd without offending it with his more libertine sensibility and predilection for alternative religion (7), even though he spent a lot of time on Christian radio shows. The Texe Marrs ministry in particular moved thousands of copies of the Black Helicopter books. Keith also began branching out to other publishers. He did a remarkable volume called Secret and Suppressed for Feral House. It continued what he did with the zines, circulating underground treatises, samizdat, theses and rants. Shortly thereafter, David Childress' Adventures Unlimited Press published Keith's *Mind Control, World Cont*rol (8).

Keith's writing schedule, in fact, seemed to multiply greatly with passing time. He virtually had become a partner to publisher Ron Bonds at IllumiNet. The Black Helicopter books began to make the national impact he wanted. Although not the first to point out the phenomenon of the black choppers, he had an early and abiding interest in it going back to the cattle mutilations of the late 1970s (9), and in his wake the black helicopter theme went into ascendancy in popular culture. Keith had appeared on a number of network television shows and also had a mounting schedule of Art Bell-level radio appearances and conference lectures. But he never got that book contract with a major publisher (10) and his name fell short in terms of wide recognition even of Bill Cooper's.

Kerry Thornley's path had long preceded Jim Keith, of course, but was similar in its tributaries from the zine scene. His involvement with Jim Garrison's 1968 investigation of the JFK case brought him some national prominence that he initially eschewed. As he recovered memories of his weird connections to the Kennedy conundrum (11), however, they became fodder for a personality he transmitted through the zines, only some of which were self-published. They included ideas about mind control and hidden history that since have gained near mainstream currency, at least in movies and TV shows.

Kerry still engenders the scorn of Garrison scholars. Many see him as one of the shadowy, perhaps guilty, parties in the web of intrigue that surrounds the JFK assassination. Others suggest that the turnaround in his attitude about that kind of notoriety reflected some cheap hustle to pump it for money and fame, neither of which he ever had in any significant amount, especially as compared to that accrued by the cowards and hustlers who really did bushwhack JFK. The flatfooted would-be investigators of this aspect of Kerry Thornley disregard his finest creative work, such as the co-founding of Discordianism, his books *Principia Discordia* and *Zenarchy*, and his latter-day *Dreadlock Recollections*; indeed, some seem unaware of it.

The straight view of Thornley is that he did have some role in the assassination and that these other things represented his way of deflecting the issue or his descent into a mishmash of pseudo-philosophy or even insanity. When I met Kerry Thornley in Atlanta in 1992, and in the conversations I had with him afterward, I witnessed no madness; quite the reverse. I also saw no seedy desire for undue fame. He told me that he happily assented to the Zen of dishwashing, his day job at the time of one of our radio interviews.

What little underground notoriety Kerry Thornley had came not from shameless self-promotion but from a genuine interest among readers in what he had to say. It was a bizarre rant but a consistent one that resonated with many other's experience of the Kennedy weirdness. Thornley's experience began before his wild rants, though and even before the Kennedy assassination itself. He wrote a novel about his Marine buddy Lee Harvey Oswald well before the assassination (12). He telegraphed Oswald, in much the same way pulp publisher Ray Palmer had telegraphed a view of Fred Crisman, as did also Jim Garrison himself (13). If this wasn't time travel, it was remarkable prescience.

Many times I had strong disagreements with both Jim Keith and Kerry Thornley. Keith really pissed me off once by circulating the information of a low-level shill who had harassed several friends and me. I did not and do not agree with Kerry Thornley's take on John Kennedy, Jim Garrison or Robert Anton Wilson – the great *Illuminatus!* satirist who Thornley at one time regarded as his CIA handler – although I can certainly understand his gripe with Garrison. Agreement has never been the point of any of this kind of writing and research. Speaking in one voice is the province of mainstream media, and, as Keith pointed out, the mainstream media speak it over and over again in the daily "news" cycles as a kind of hypnotic mass mind control. Neither Keith nor Kerry were ever short of conflicting arguments and ideas "that there may ever continue more than one life-line back into a Past we risk, each day, losing our forbears in forever." (14) Jim

Commander X's Guide to Incredible Conspiracies

Keith and Kerry Thornley have become if not forbears of a free-thought underground, at least two remarkable personalities who passed on its baton to others.

(1) Sheriff deputies killed Cooper in Eager, Arizona in 2001, after he resisted arrest on public endangerment charges indirectly linked to his federal tax resistance.

(2) At the Coalition of Political Assassinations conference in November 2002, comedian/activist/philosopher Dick Gregory called **Behold A Pale Horse**, "a great book." While not a terribly penetrating analysis of the book, the fact that such a respected personality made the comment before an assembled group of the most serious researchers on the JFK/RFK/MLK assassinations so long after Cooper's death testifies to its durability.

(3) Cooper and I once spoke at the same UFO conference in Las Vegas. The conference lectures served as commercials for later workshops that had separate registration fees. At the time, Cooper had abandoned many of his claims about the government working in tandem with evil aliens under the MAJESTYTWELVE program and had started on a direction toward many of the themes of the burgeoning militia movement. He called his audience a bunch of "ufoologists" and otherwise threw epithets and insults at it. Nevertheless, a huge line formed to get into his workshop. In contrast, my rather academic discourse on Wilhelm Reich's 1950s battles with UFOs in the desert southwest drew a crowd of about six people.

(4) These included latter-day Situationists, Subgenius church members, No Work/Free Rent people, communists and anarchists of various stripes, and Erisian chaos worshippers as well as Kerry Thornley himself. The milieu was quite different from the various UFO organizations with its network of MUFON and NICAP type organizations, adding wild tangents to material like Paul Bennewitz' rants regarding the alien-human factories in Dulce, New Mexico, which may have had some influence on the likes of Bill Cooper. The Bennewitz story is told fully now in the book **The Bennewitz Affair**, by Keith friend Greg Bishop.

(5) **The Gemstone File** is a chronology of information regarding the unusual line of thinking that Aristotle Onassis kidnapped Howard Hughes and absconded with his empire. It includes the notion that the international mob under Onassis killed JFK. Following Keith's lead, I compiled a comprehensive collection of Gemstone history in a book entitled **Inside the Gemstone File**.

(6) Instead, this task fell to Keith's friend Len Bracken, who compiled and wrote **The Shadow Government, 9/11 and State Terror**.

(7) Keith belonged to the Church of Scientology for eighteen years. He repudiated it, though, and even skewered William Bramley's book **Gods of Eden** in Steamshovel Press for what he perceived as its Scientology subtext. Shortly before he died, Keith expressed some interest in the self-help cult, Avatar.

(8) AUP has begun to issue new editions of Keith's IllumiNet books, including the classic **Saucers of the Illuminati**. The pre-IllumiNet edition of that one may have been Keith's last zine, a spiral bound, photocopy edition done under the pseudonym Jay Katz. I wrote a new foreword to the post-IllumiNet edition.

(9) Keith noted in FATE magazine that most of the carcasses of cattle apparently picked up and dumped off by the black helicopters contained unusual amounts of clostridium bacteria, something also pointed out by the writer Ed Sanders. In the new edition of the book I co-wrote with Keith, **The Octopus** (Feral House, 2003), I include a

chapter about the connection between Keith's death-and that of IllumiNet's Ron Bonds—and clostridium.

More recently, some note has been made that Keith's death certificate listed the cause as "blunt force trauma". Keith officially died of a pulmonary embolism resulting from a knee injury at the Burning Man festival, however, which may have been the meaning of this reference.

(10) Book publishing is a major conspiracy between publishers and the book buyers of the various chains. A major publisher announces that hundreds of thousands of copies of a book will be produced and the book buyers translate that into hundreds of thousands of dollars to be sunk into the promotion of the book. Therefore, they increase their orders for the books by the hundreds of thousands. This kind of flooding of the marketplace leaves little room for the smaller efforts with the more interesting ideas.

(11) Beginning this process is the great favor Jim Garrison did for Kerry Thornley, although Thornley never acknowledged it as such.

(12) Kerry Thornley's ***The Idle Warriors***, written in 1962, was published for the first time by IllumiNet Press in 1991. IllumiNet also published editions of ***Zenarchy*** and ***Principia Discordia***. Kerry's connection to the Garrison case has been the subject of one book, but his first comprehensive biography, ***The Prankster and the Conspiracy*** (Paraview Press, 2003), was written by Jim Keith compatriot Adam Gorightly.

(13) The full story told in Maury Island UFO.

(14) Thomas Pynchon, Mason & Dixon.

Jim Keith and Kerry Thornley both appeared in the conspiracy magazine ***Steamshovel Press***, which continues to showcase the best in parapolitical writing. Single issues cost $7 and four issue subscriptions cost $25, from POB 210553, St. Louis, MO 63121. Checks and money orders should be payable to "Kenn Thomas" not "Steamshovel Press."

Commander X's Guide to Incredible Conspiracies

The Strange Death of James Forrestal
By Peter Robbins

James Forrestal was a man whose influence, policies and very presence dominated much of what was the news from 1940 until 1949, but ask the average American who he was and they will likely draw a blank, and with good cause. Excluding a handful of noteworthy exceptions, this former Secretary of the Navy, former Secretary of Defense and a key architect of our modern defense establishment, has effectively been written out of the history books and our national consciousness, an Orwellian bit of historical revisionism if ever there was one. How and why did this quiet purge occur, and how does it relate to the classified, UFO-related history of postwar America? Did the man who created our modern Department of Defense take his own life, or was it taken from him?

Officially, early on the morning of May 22, 1949, he fell to his death from a sixteenth story window at the Bethesda Naval Hospital where he was being treated for depression. But this account does not hold up under study of the evidence at hand, which while circumstantial, points toward murder.

Forrestal's death was precipitated by a profound nervous breakdown, brought on no doubt by a combination of factors. He was a complex, driven individual who over the years assumed tremendous responsibilities in his public life while his private life suffered. I think there was a central factor in his emotional collapse, and it had to do with the unique gravity of the situation he inherited when he was sworn in as America's first Secretary of Defense on September 17, 1947. Before any case can or should be made, the reader needs to have some appreciation of who this man was, even if in bullet points:

· Born into Irish-American family in 1892 in Dutchess County New York, his father a contractor active in local Democratic Party activities, his mother a teacher at a nearby Catholic school.
· Attended Dartmouth 1911, transferred to Princeton in 1912.
· Left Princeton three weeks prior to graduating to join Wall Street brokerage firm, then enlisted in Navy in 1916.
· Trained to be flier but armistice precluded his seeing action.
· Returned to States late 1918 and the employ of same firm. Became partner in 1923 and President in 1926. Same year married Vogue writer and former Zigfield showgirl Josephine Ogden.
· Prospered on Wall Street through the Depression.
· Couple had two sons but neither proved very good at parenting. Both have affairs and take lovers.
· Forrestal's financial skills brought to attention of Franklin Roosevelt who invited him to join select group of business leaders who advised President on economic matters. Forrestal took call to public service seriously, put his business life on hold and moved to Washington.
· Appointed Under Secretary of Navy in May 1940 and soon directing and overseeing manufacture and flow of all the Navy's war needs, superbly, by all accounts.
· Sworn in as Secretary of Navy in 1940, began to keep diary same year.
· As Navy Secretary puts himself in harm's way more than once and is present at Battles of Laiti Gulf, the Solomons and Normandy Invasion.

· Becomes Administration's point man in securing and finalizing so-called Lend Lease Agreement by which British were advanced millions of tons of badly-needed war material.

· Served with distinction throughout the war.

· Following secession of hostilities, Truman asked the Army and Navy to submit plans for unification of the armed forces.

· Truman favored Navy's plan and appointed Forrestal to head up creation of a new Department of Defense. Forrestal saw job through to successful completion despite ongoing inter-service rivalries.

On June 24, 1947 Kenneth Arnold's Washington State UFO sighting became the subject of international press coverage and initiated the so-called modern age of UFOs. Then, on or about the fourth of July, something, or things, crashed in the plains of New Mexico less than eighty miles from Roswell, home of the world's only atomic bomb wing. Forty-eight hours later the story was international news.

The National Security Act was passed by Congress on July 26 and the President immediately named Forrestal as Secretary of Defense. Passage of the Act also brought into existence that July the National Security Council, the Joint Chiefs of Staff, the Central Intelligence Agency and Dr. Vannavar Bush's Research and Development Board.

Secretary of Defense

Then on September 17, 1947 in route from a state visit to Brazil, President Truman sent a message instructing that Forrestal be sworn in immediately. Why? General Twining's "Air Material Command Opinion Concerning Flying Discs," is dated only six days later and states "The phenomenon reported is something real and not visionary or fictitious." That same day, September 23, Forrestal arrived at his new offices in the Pentagon. The next day was September 24.

The Eisenhower Briefing Document of November 18, 1952 is generally considered the least controversial of the so-called MJ-12 documents, but if authentic confirms at the least, U.S. awareness of an extraterrestrial presence, the crash at Roswell, and creation on September 24, 1947 of "a TOP SECRET Research and Development Intelligence operation responsible directly and only to the President of the United States." James Forrestal is listed as number three of the twelve men named to this group.

The Briefing Document came with a one page attachment that authorized the new Defense Secretary to proceed "with all due speed and caution upon your undertaking." Three days later Forrestal issued his first directive as Secretary of Defense and the Air Force is activated.

On January 7, 1948 Captain Thomas Mantell and two other Kentucky Air National Guard pilots were scrambled after a UFO "of tremendous size" was reported in the skies near Fort Knox. Mantell was killed when his plane exploded in an uncontrolled descent.

By Mid-October 1948 victory seemed all but assured for the Republican Presidential candidate Thomas E. Dewey. Forrestal confided to a friend that he was deeply concerned that "since Dewey might be elected President, his representatives should be briefed in preparation for the possibility." But his common sense proposal drew the resentment of Administration officials who equated it with disloyalty to the President.

Commander X's Guide to Incredible Conspiracies

By late November, James Forrestal's star was in decline at the White House.

Forrestal tendered his resignation on March 3 and met with Truman on the 10th. At that time the Secretary requested that White House personnel take possession of his multi-thousand page 'diary, given the amount of classified material it contained. The White House acquiesces.

The Breakdown

On March 28, the day of his retirement, Forrestal joined Defense Department employees assembled to see his replacement sworn in. President Truman presented the retiring Secretary with the Distinguished Service Metal, the highest civilian decoration authorized by Congress. Unable to respond to the President's generous words of praise, he was lead speechless from the room.

Following the ceremonies, Air Force Secretary Stuart Symington, who had regularly challenged Forrestal's authority, spoke with him and the effect on Forrestal was deeply upsetting, if not traumatic. He was found at his desk several hours later staring at the wall and repeating the phrase "you are a loyal fellow. You are a loyal fellow..."

He was driven back to his Georgetown home where his friend Ferdinand Eberstadt arrived soon afterwards. Eberstadt was taken aback by his old friend's manner and recalled Forrestal telling him that he was a total failure and considering suicide. It seemed Forrestal was also convinced that certain persons in the White House had formed a conspiracy to "get him" and had finally succeeded.

On April 2, Forrestal and Eberstadt flew to Florida where their friend Robert Lovett had an estate. Over the next three days Forrestal attempted to take his life several times and the Navy sends Captain George M. Raines to Florida. Raines is Chief of Neuro Psychiatry at the Bethesda Naval Hospital in Maryland. But an examination would have to wait. Forrestal's family had asked Dr. William C. Menninger to be psychiatrist of record, and as such Raines was duty-bound to wait until Menninger arrived the next day.

Bethesda

The following afternoon the doctors examined the patient, consulted, and concluded the best course of action was confinement at Bethesda Naval Hospital. Menninger, now officially Forrestal's Psychiatrist then flew back to his clinic, and while regularly briefed, never saw his patient again.

Dr. Raines accompanied Forrestal from Florida to Maryland and on the drive from the airfield to the hospital Forrestal had to be restrained to keep him from throwing himself from the moving car. Once admitted and secured in a room on the sixteenth floor, a twenty-four hour Marine guard was put on his door. For much of the first month he was kept heavily sedated.

A week passed with no mention of Forrestal's breakdown or hospitalization in the press or on the radio. The New York Times first ran the story on April 8 and noted that doctors were "very much encouraged by the former Defense Secretary's response to care."

One of the first people Forrestal called when he was allowed phone privileges was Monsignor Maurice J. Sheehy, a highly regarded prelate at the Catholic University in Washington. Although he has drifted from the church over the years, Forrestal asked the

Monsignor to help him return to it. Sheehy of course agreed and planned an initial visit to Bethesda.

While at Bethesda, Forrestal phoned the White House insistent that someone be sent over to check for a bug (listening device) in the wall of his room. The White House sent Sidney Souers, the first Secretary of the National Security Council and a future Director of the Central Intelligence Agency. Admiral Souers was one of the Harry Truman's closest confidants and advisors.

Secretary of Defense Louis Johnson visited Forrestal on April 27 and reported his predecessor looked fine and "should be out of the hospital in two to three weeks." Also on April 27 the Air Force distributed copies of "Project Saucer" to the press, its desensitized civilian version of Project SIGN.

On May 17 the Times reported that Forrestal has gained twelve pounds since being confined on April 2. By that time visitors and hospital personnel alike seemed in agreement that the Secretary's condition was improving.

Henry Forrestal decided that his brother should complete his recovery privately in the countryside and made plans to travel to Washington on May 22. He telephoned hospital administrators on May 20 and informed them that he would be taking custody of his brother on Sunday May 22.

Monsignor Sheehy had now called at Bethesda Naval Hospital on six separate occasions but was told each time that Forrestal was unable to see him. Increasingly frustrated, the Monsignor made an appointment to speak with Secretary of Navy John Sullivan and the two met on May 20. Sullivan in turn contacted Bethesda and was given assurances that Sheehy would be able to see the patient in time, but not enough time as it turned out. James Forrestal had two days left to live.

Official accounts of Forrestal's death vary slightly but follow this basic line: While staff psychiatrist Commander R.R. Deen was asleep in the room next to Forrestal's, an attendant, Hospital Apprentice R.W. Harrison, looked in on the Secretary at about 1:45AM to find the patient awake and copying a Sophocles poem out of a poetry anthology.

Harrison asked Forrestal if he would like a sleeping pill but it was declined. Harrison then reported to Commander Deen's room (though according to another account he reported to the hospital security station on another floor) and updated the officer on the patient's condition. Harrison allegedly forgot to lock Forrestal's door behind him at 1:45. When he checked the room again at 1:50 it was empty and a search commenced.

The seventh floor duty nurse then reported hearing a loud sound from her window. It was the sound of Forrestal's body hitting the third floor roof. Hospital authorities surmised the patient, finding his door unlocked, walked across the hall to the efficiency kitchen, pushed open the unsecured screen window, knotted his bathrobe sash tightly around his neck, tied the free end to the radiator below the window, then lowered himself out of the window and was killed when the knot at the radiator end of the sash slipped its mooring.

Newspapers worldwide headlined the tragedy on May 23. Two days later Josephine Forrestal returned to Washington from Paris where she had been for the entire duration of her husband's illness. Her first public act was to absolve everyone of blame in her husband's death, this without benefit of even a cursory investigation. That afternoon with six thousand in attendance, James Forrestal was buried at Arlington Cemetery with full military honors, including a nineteen Howitzer salute. He was fifty-seven years old.

Commander X's Guide to Incredible Conspiracies

July 19th's *New York Times* reported that: "Considerable mystery surrounds a delay in releasing the report made by the special naval investigating board that inquired into the death of James V. Forrestal. Naval press officers gave the impression that at least a summary of his finding would be made public."

The board began its hearings on May 23 but concluded them after only seven days. For the next two weeks Navy and National Military Establishment press sections promised to release the report but did not.

On September 23rd, the public first learned of the existence of Forrestal's diary and that it was being held at the White House for safekeeping. It was described as filling an entire filing cabinet and included copies of numerous SECRET and TOP SECRET classified documents.

On October 11 Navy Secretary Matthews made public the investigating board's report absolving "all" of any blame in Forrestal's death, and in no uncertain terms: "That the death was not caused in any manner by the intent, fault, negligence or inefficiency of any person or persons in the naval service or connected therewith." Such language suggests the Navy was more concerned with protecting itself than pursuing the matter actually under investigation.

The report concluded that 1. The body found on the third floor ledge was Forrestal's, 2. that he died of injuries sustained in the fall, 3. that his behavior prior to death "was indicative of a mental depression," and 4. "that the treatment and precautions in the conduct of the case were in agreement with accepted psychiatric practice and commensurate with the evident status of the patient at all times."

Driving home the 'casualty of war'/'occupational fatigue' rationale by both government and media greatly helped Americans accept Forrestal's death as a suicide and there was little cause to feel otherwise. And give or take, this 'operational fatigue' can be traced to the time he was sworn in as Secretary of Defense.

Forrestal's friend, Pulitzer Prize-winning journalist Arthur Krock, recalled "From the time of his appointment as Secretary of Defense in 1947, my wife had begun to detect inner disturbances in Forrestal that I had not." And writing in late 1949, columnist Drew Pearson noted in his memoirs that: "the Defense Secretary's nervous deterioration dated back over two years." Both observations, one from a good friend, the other from an outspoken enemy, support the fact that Forrestal's mental problems began at about the time he was sworn in.

The Forrestal 'Diary

In 1951 the Viking Press published a massively edited version of Forrestal's diaries that quickly became a national best-seller. *The Times* characterized it as "...a wealth of observations made just prior to and after World War II by a man who, aside from standing at the center of great events, was acknowledged to be an accurate observer of the history of his time." Its five hundred eighty one pages were drawn from the over twenty eight hundred pages alleged to be the full extent of Forrestal's writings. But a September 23rd 1949 article in *The Times* stated that: "The journal fills a whole filing cabinet, it is said, and is accompanied by many documents that still are stamped top secret." It takes a lot more than twenty eight hundred pages to fill a standard four or five drawer filing cabinet, and fifteen to twenty thousand pages is a more realistic estimate of the diary's actual size.

Commander X's Guide to Incredible Conspiracies

Murder or Suicide

New York Times Features reporter Walter H. Waggoner was the lead journalist assigned to the story immediately following the tragedy. Within hours of Forrestal's plunge Waggoner established the following:

1. "The sash of his dressing-gown was still knotted and wrapped tightly around his neck when he was found, but hospital officials would not speculate as to its purpose."

2. "Mr. Forrestal had copied most of the Sophocles poem from the book, but he had apparently been interrupted in his efforts. His copying stopped after he had written "night" of the word "nightingale."

3. "Reports from his doctors and hospital authorities had indicated steady progress toward his recovery."

4. "It had been accepted that continued treatment would have brought Mr. Forrestal to complete recovery in a matter of months."

5. "On the window sill from which Mr. Forrestal jumped were marks suggesting he might have changed his mind and tried to climb back in the window."

Why was Hospital Apprentice R.W. Harrison, who had never had any previous contact with Forrestal, assigned to him on this particular night? One account has it that the regularly assigned attendant did not appear for his shift due to drunkenness, something which had never happened before.

Then there is the matter of Monsignor Sheehy. Forrestal had expressed a desire to return to the Church, and by implication the sanctity of the confessional. From the point of view of anyone who considered Forrestal a security risk or potential security risk, Father Sheehy would have been the last person the Secretary should have been allowed to speak with. And in six attempts to see him, The Monsignor never got beyond the reception area.

On May 20, Henry Forrestal informed the naval hospital that he intended to take his brother out of Bethesda on Sunday May 22 to recuperate privately. Following James' death that morning, Henry became convinced that his brother had been murdered, and he wasn't alone in this belief.

Arnold A. Rogow's book, *James Forrestal: A Study of Personality, Politics and Policy* is a scholarly and insightful work for which the author interviewed many who were closest to Forrestal, including Dean Atchison, Clark Clfford, Louis Johnson, Robert Lovett, Arthur Krock, Henry Forrestal, Dr.William Menninger, Dr. George Raines and Harry S. Truman. Rogow was anything but a conspiracist, but early on in his narrative writes, "Officially of course, Forrestal committed suicide on May 22, 1949, but among those close to him, there are even a few that are certain he was murdered, or if not murdered, that his death was very much desired by individuals and groups who in 1949 held great power in the United States."

Aftermath

In assuming the mantle of Secretary of Defense, James Forrestal was charged with being "the principle assistant to the President in all matters relating to national security" (emphasis mine). He had authority to establish military policy and programs and held power over all the service branches. Yet despite every conceivable effort, the military forces he commanded remained unable to either confront or gain significant knowledge of the aerial unknowns.

Fifty-five years ago this dedicated public servant broke under the strain of combined factors, not the least of which was his first-hand knowledge that the most powerful nation on Earth was powerless in the face of an unknown threat. He died seven weeks after suffering a nervous breakdown, was buried, eulogized, then pretty much forgotten.

I think many of us imagine that for the sufferer, an emotional breakdown is marked by internal confusion and clouded thinking. In fact the central experience of such a dysfunction may be a terrible sense of clarity, real or imagined, about the causal circumstances of ones' undoing. I am convinced that once James Forrestal broke under the strain, he saw the writing on the wall and knew that if he did not 'do the right thing,' that is kill himself, that others would certainly do it for him. But once his darkest days began to fall away however and the prescribed therapy actually began to produce results, the patient on the sixteenth floor grew stronger and began to recover his sense of self, and his will to live. This turn of events seem to have sealed his fate.

To that select group who held power in this country at the middle of the last century, James Forrestal's mental collapse had to be treated as a priority national security matter: the man knew everything and might say anything. The decision to force him out of that window was in no way personal. The murder of James Forrestal was simply the only way to guarantee the resolution of what this group had come to perceive as a potential security risk of the first magnitude.

The fact is, history has shown James Forrestal to have been a true patriot in word and deed, but when he was interred at Arlington National Cemetery, more than his body was laid to rest. His name and accomplishments have been almost entirely erased from the history of the Twentieth Century, a history that for better or worse, he had a great deal to do with shaping, and that is something that should be corrected.

Do we have enough evidence to establish that our first Secretary of Defense was murdered? No, not yet.

References:

1. "The Forrestal Diaries," Millus, Walter, Editor, Viking Press 1951
2. James Forrestal: Driven Patriot by Townsend Hoppes, Knopf, 1992
3. "Floating Mystery Ball Is New Nazi Air Weapon," New York Times, December 14, 1944
4. "'Flying Disks' Fail To Stir Air Forces," NY Times, July 4, 1947
5. "Unification Act Signed," NY Times, July 27, 1947
6. "Forrestal is Sworn in Suddenly," NY Times, September 18, 1947
7. "Wallace Criticizes Truman Order On Rush Swearing In of Forrestal," NY Times, September 17, 1947
8. Demands Truman Tell What Emergency Caused Haste in Swearing In Forrestal," NY Times, September 19, 1947
9. Eisenhower Briefing Document of November 18, 1952, 8 pages
10. Memorandum from the President to Secretary Truman, September 24, 1947
11. "Spaatz Will Head Our New Air Force, President also appoints Bush to be Chairman of the Research and Development Board," NY Times, 11/26/47

12. "New Air Unit Operating," NY Times, September 28, 1947

13. UFOs and the National Security State, Dolan, Richard, Hampton Roads Publishing Co., 2002

14. Memoirs, Krock Arthur, Funk & Wagnalls, 1968

15. FBI Memorandum to J. Edgar Hoover, January 31, 1949

16. USAF Incoming Classified Message, January 31, 1949

17. Project SIGN, February 1949, page 25

18. "Thousands Look On As New Defense Secretary Takes Oath," NY Times, March 29, 1949

19. "Forrestal Gets Distinguished Service Metal; Outgoing Secretary Speechless at Surprise," NY Times, March 29, 1949

20. Counsel To the President, Clifford Clark with Richard Holbrooke, Random House, 1991

21. "Forrestal Is Treated in Naval Hospital For Nervous and Physical Exhaustion, " NY Times, April 8, 1949

22. "Forrestal 'Looks Fine," NY Times, April 27, 1949

23. "Forrestal Killed in 13-Story Leap; U.S. Mourning Set, Nation Is Shocked," NY Times, May 23, 1949

24. "Hospital Absolved By Mrs. Forrestal," NY Times, May 26, 1949

25. July 18, "Forrestal Data Held Up - Report on His Death Promised but It Is Not Released," NY Times, July 19 1949

26. "White House Holds Forrestal's Diary: First Defense Secretary Sent Journal, Much Top Secret, There For Safekeeping," NY Times, September 22, 1949

27. "Navy Absolves All In Forrestal Leap," NY Times, October 12, 1949

28. James Forrestal: A Study of Personality, Politics and Policy, Arnold A. Rogow, Macmillan, 1963

The Strange Death of James Forrestal - Working draft for *Phenomenon Magazine*
By Peter Robbins - Copyright 2004 Peter Robbins

Commander X's Guide to Incredible Conspiracies

UNDERGROUND BASES AND INNER EARTH MYSTERIES

Alien Installations and Underground Bases
By Christi Verismo

AUTHOR'S NOTE: This report results from two years of part time investigation of recent developments in Australia which appear to indicate that some unusual and urgent preparations are being made to turn Australia into a self sufficient "safe haven."

Australia's UFO Connections

An article was sent to the Rumor Mills news site anonymously about recent developments in Australia preparing it to be a safe haven for the global elite during a One World Government with martial law. An alien invasion may also be impending. http://rumormillnews.com/FORTRESS_AUSTRALIA.htm. It appears to be written by an Australian former government insider. Here is a short summary.

In 1989 Australian emergency services began to be upgraded and military reservists encouraged and the National Safety Council was started for this (NSCA). Police, Fire and Ambulance services are now under one roof and sold to a company called 'Intergraph Inc' which is a specialized American communications company said to be closely connected to the NSA.

In 1976 an American John Fredrich, backed by the CIA joined and became executive director in 1982. It expanded rapidly with an elaborate base in Gippsland, Victoria containing a private air force and marine section. Australian intelligence were trained by the CIA. NSCA provided security back up to all the American secret bases in Australia including the new Omega bases in Victoria and Tasmania.

The U.S. Air force conducted joint training exercises with the NSCA. The association with the East Sale secure RAAF base was a close one and is often used by NASA U2 flights and other unexplained U.S. aircraft. It is also the repository of secret UFO information and Frederick Valentich attended for a special course relating to UFOs before he disappeared over Bass Strait in 1978 while reporting a close encounter with a large UFO.

So concerned was Valentich about what he had seen and been told at Sale that he emotionally told his parents shortly afterwards that "should they take me I should be O.K. so don't worry, they will probably put me back."

NSCA is said to be closely involved with the UFO problem and can effect retrievals on land and from the great ocean depths. Their private airline for did drug running and moving laundered money in and out of Australia. Freidrich flew in an executive jet in U.S. colors and the CIA insignia on the tail and his ex personal pilot mentioned three occasions he collected him from Pine Gap where was always waiting alone on the vacant airstrip.

A new headquarters is being selected near Canberra probably in underground facilities in the Snowy Mountains. It is a vast system capable of supporting thousands of people and connected to Canberra by a secret, underground railway. There is now an integrated military force that is coordinated with all emergency services and police organizations. The machinery of a police state is firmly in place and total military control could be established in a few hours. In 1996 the Australian army, air force and navy were coordinated under a single Commanding officer. New training methods for the police have been adopted and 'state of the art' equipment purchased.

The FBI has been helping restructure in line with the American system. This includes specialized training courses in 'Advanced Interrogation Methods.' Wackenhut Inc, owned by a former FBI senior officer that is still in contact with them and the CIA, is privatizing Australian prisons.

Rumors persist of internment camps in prohibited military areas. Wackenhut Inc is supplying hundreds of kit form tent prisons, razor wire and electric fencing. In 1975 Prime Minister Whitlam resented America's secret bases at Pine gap, Narrunga and NW Cape.

Ironically Pine Gap helped Whitlam's removal by carrying secret communications between Washington and Australia. The spy Christopher Boyce read the top-secret coded traffic going to and coming from Pine Gap that indicated that America was destroying the Australian Govt. His supervisor, named the Governor General, who sacked Whitlam as 'our man Kerr'. Boyce saw daily instructions sent to C.I.A. field officers, Australian union leaders, politicians, senior public officials and many others on the payroll. Pine Gap made it easy.

The deputy P.M. Dr. Jim Cairns, claimed the Americans would mount a violent overthrow of the government if they did not succeed by clandestine means. Saying 'I believe there is a strong chance the Americans will try to do to us what they have just done in Chile, we could all be killed in the process.' He was serious.

The Pine Gap Operation

A scientist among Australia's elite in a key position revealed: There are at least ten top-secret American facilities in Australia with the so called 'Joint defense Space Research Facility' at Pine Gap being the most important.

Originally Pine Gap was decreed to control and act as a downlink for geosynchronous satellites gathering intelligence, stationed over the Pacific and Asia by the CIA, NSA and the NRO. Pine Gap's position is for its proximity to the Pacific and Indian Oceans and Asia, and window to outer space. Its position on the earth's surface in relation to other important areas situated on the planet, its isolation and situation in an area of low electromagnetic radiation. Construction was undertaken entirely by American contractors who flew in their own workforce from the US on a shift basis. The base became operational after two years.

Large underground facilities are rumored to extend some twelve levels below the base. Long tunnels are laid out in a pattern similar to the spokes of a wheel and extend several miles from the center of the base. In a deep-shielded underground chamber a secret nuclear reactor similar in size to those used to power submarines was installed to drive large AC and DC generators. It also has an 'official' above ground diesel powered generating station that is not connected to an outside electricity supply.

Reportedly, extending some 20,000 below the base is a bore-hole containing an ultra low frequency antenna which is apparently used for secret experiments supposedly related to Nicola Tesla's resonance theories as well as low frequency communications throughout the world. Pine Gap's communication systems are the most sophisticated available utilizing satellites, microwave, low frequency and their own dedicated cable to the USA.

They are directly connected to Nurrunga, North West Cape, Geraldton, Australian Defence Signals Directorate in Melbourne, Canberra, Sydney, all CIA and NSA stations, ASIO, SIS and the Australian Defence Science and Technology Organisation which deals with UFOs and crash retrievals.

Weekly personal shopping is undertaken in the U.S.A. Pine Gap is a multi-billion dollar operation of great importance to the American government. Pine Gap has eight white radomes placed near groups of long low buildings.

A few miles from the base has a double security fence patrolled continuously by American guards and the Australian Federal Police Force. Pine Gap is now being expanded. A second above ground power station is now under construction as well as a large number of houses for additional staff. The staff was increased to around 1,200 in 1996. The reason given is "Asian economic espionage".

UFOs Seen Near Pine Gap

The Fortress Australia writer says Central and South Australia has always had high UFO activity focusing on the Woomers rocket-range and the nuclear test site at Maralinga. Since construction started at Pine Gap and later at Nurrunga, there was a rapid rise in UFO sightings, which have continued, some being described as bizarre.

One case in 1989 involved three hunters who were on an all night shooting trip in the hills near Pine Gap. At around 4.30a.m. they observed a large camouflaged door open on the side of a low hill inside the security compound and a metallic, circular disc appear from the gaping black hole, tip on its edge and disappear vertically at tremendous speed. The door then slowly shut and everything returned to normal. The camouflage was so good that from their vantage point they were unable to observe anything unusual about the area after the door closed.

In 1975 the occupants of a passenger plane which was passing, observed a large white object, similar in size to one of the white radomes, suddenly leapt into the air and disappeared rapidly towards the north west. Most of the passengers and crew witnessed the event.

In 1980 a camouflaged door case occurred when two members of the Northern Territory Police, who were taking part in a search for a missing Alice Springs child, watched as three 'bath tub' shaped objects flew slowly over the base and then one by one disappeared in to an oblong black hole in a hillside. This also occurred during the early hours of the morning and as the two police officers had arranged to meet other members of the search party they left without seeing the door close.

In 1973 another type of sighting involves, blue, red and gold pencil like beams. A man camped near Pine Gap saw a vertical shaft of very bright blue light emanating from the area of the base.   His binoculars showed most of the base, 8 miles away as well as a strange looking object apparently hovering above it at a height he estimated to be around one thousand feet.

Firstly he thought it was a cigar shaped balloon or blimp but this idea quickly evaporated when the object slowly tipped to a 45-degree angle exposing what appeared to be its top surface. The object was perfectly circular with a central dome. 1000 feet above the base the cartographer estimated the diameter of the disc to be a little more than half the distance between the Pine Gap base and the disc's bottom edge, making it between

500/600 ft in diameter. In the moonlight the disc appeared to be a dull grey color with a light yellow fuzz around its edge. A thin bright blue beam, like a rod, slowly extended from the disc to the base – it slowly moved in a telescopic fashion from the disc and gradually extended behind the radomes.

A few minutes later the light beam retracted only to be followed by a similar blue beam slowly extending from the base to the disc. Followed by a gold colored beam that appeared very close to the blue one. After about thirty seconds both retracted back into the base.

This process continued for about forty minutes and ended when the disc made some rapid oscillations 'lit up like a neon sign' and ascended vertically at very high speed, disappearing in a few seconds. After he reported it he got a 'grilling' by some very officious people who warned him to keep silent about his experience otherwise he would be in for some very real trouble.

Alien Contacts

The Fortress Australia writer claims alien contact was possibly first achieved by the USA, with information from various sources indicating radio communication followed by personal contact occurred in the early 1950's. The Soviet Union and UK established their own contacts about the same time.

After some understanding was reached the initial methods of communication were centralized in the USA with the Russians co-operating by the mid-1950s. This developed the secret establishment of the NSA by the Truman administration in November, 1954 to identify, monitor and establish reliable and secure communications with visiting aliens with which they are now deeply involved.

The aliens are pursuing their own agendas and reject interference from earth's officialdom or the broad masses they control. Alien involvement in Australia is similar to that of the USA, Europe and Russia. For some technological rewards and minor co-operation in other areas the E.T.'s conduct their own genetic experimentation and the exploitation of the country is generally totally unhindered by humans. They do what they want, as there is no way of stopping them.

During the 1950's and early 1960's the British were conducting nuclear testing in South Australia, test firing a variety of missiles at the Woomera Rocket Range. The UFO activity was so intense that it had to be suspended, often for several days, due to electromagnetic effects causing total electrical failure at the test sights. Woomera itself was often blacked out for hours by the close approach of the UFOs.

More than sixteen thousand feet of film was taken of a variety of vehicles crisscrossing the area. During the early 1950s both the USA and Russia made contact with two alien species that apparently often worked together on various scientific projects and joint military matters.

As many as seven other groups were visiting the planet not associated with the first two. They were unfriendly to them and each other and often directly hostile to humans. Secret official research at the time indicated that several of these groups appeared to be preparing a huge world wide military operation or police action against the earth. So friendly co-operation with the first two groups became even more important. Technical help provided by the two initial contact groups brought accelerated technology and made the development of SDI a real possibility. In return for our governments allowing these aliens secret exploitation of the planet and human race, they would provide the technical know how to prevent further major wars and stop any other interested extraterrestrials from invading the planet.

It has been said with some authority that they are the brains behind SDI (Star Wars) the extension of which is HAARP that is aimed at creating an electromagnetic shield around the world to prevent an attack from outer space. The Russians have actively co-operated since its inception.

Such advanced defense systems required world wide coverage involving operational centers in secure areas in several countries. Australia is utilized for this purpose. Pine Gap involves secret scientific experiments into anti gravity and magnetic propulsion. Though its communication functions are important its research and developments sections situated below the surface are considered vital to the future of the planet. Here extraterrestrials conduct their work in partial co-operation with human scientists. They live in special conditions in virtual isolation and come and go as they please.

The final stages of SDI including the HAARP system should be functioning by 1998/99 and if necessary its entire worldwide operation will be controllable from the network of secret bases in Australia. We can only guess who controls it.

UFO Accidentally Seen In Hangar

The Fortress Australia writer also said the East Sale RAAF base in Victoria, NASA makes extensive use of the facilities on a regular basis and many other American and foreign nationality aircraft have been seen there along with other strange aircraft operating mainly at night time, which appear like American Stealth fighter planes.

Since the late 1940's, in co-operation with the United States and other major world government authorities East Sale has become a major UFO research establishment including crash retrievals. During the 1980's four people from a TV station attended the opening of a building at RAAF East Sale. One such hanger had two side doors were partly open so they decided to take a look inside.

Towards the rear of the hanger was a large metallic grey disc like object standing on three short legs. It was about sixty feet in diameter with a central height of about eighteen to twenty feet. Scaffolding was arranged around the objects right hand side with a platform extending to what looked like a curved doorway situated near the top of the object. They also noticed what appeared to be small square windows on each side of the doorway and evenly spaced around the top of the object.

They videotaped it noticing surface markings similar to Korean script. There was an elderly man talking to two smaller men, the size of five-year-old children in the center of the office area. They were looking at drawings on a small table and didn't notice the cameramen. The tall man looked up and appeared puzzled by the two cameramen. He walked to the door and asked them if HQ needed more pictures and why hadn't they called him about it. The TV men replied that they had nothing to do with HQ. The man's expression had absolute horror. The intruders met four guards who confiscated the film.

Has Hubble Spotted an Alien Invation?

The Tidbinbilla tracking station, jointly established between UK, USA and

Commander X's Guide to Incredible Conspiracies

Australia close to Canberra is the most important in Australia. It is a vital control center for the Hubble orbital telescope.

The first images received by Tidbinbilla found that virtually every star has a solar system. The truth angered the American control-room staff that the Australians and British now knew. Hubble now operates satisfactorily and photographs are airbrushed before release.

The Parks Radio telescopes according to a government source first detected intelligent signals from outer space more than twenty-five years ago. It has been involved with the SETI program. Parks hit rate was alarmingly high so the plug had to be pulled in 1995 before too much leaked out. Intelligent radio and television signals were identified in several parts of the galaxy and emanating from areas up to three thousand light years away from the earth. It's classified above top secret that technical civilizations equal or superior to our own were very active more than three thousand years ago. They captured enhanced television pictures showing the daily lives of a number of alien civilizations of ages past and still do.

NSA has close co-operation with Parks and has liaison staff posted there on a full time basis, as an outpost of the NSA's vital intelligence gathering network. Nothing is sure, only that obvious and massive preparations are being made to protect and secure the Australian continent from a cataclysmic event. No doubt time will tell.

The Fortress Australia author would like to mention that as far as possible the information contained in this report was checked and where possible attempts were made to verify it. However it has to be borne in mind that some information may contain some inaccuracies due to the impossibility of verifying source material. Never the less, the author considers the majority of the information well founded and truthful.

It should also be pointed out that many of the providers of this information required their identities to be covered in such a way that they could not be identified. This involved some minor alterations to the narrative to produce such cover and has not compromised the information described in any way. Rumors have persisted in Australia that all the initial SDI experiments and developments were successful and a large part of the system is fully operated and controlled by America's secret Australian and Antarctic bases.

Pine Gap Installation

Commander X's Guide to Incredible Conspiracies

The Underworld Empire
By Branton

In the April 1963 issue of **SEARCH** Magazine, Will Carson and Jeannie Joy, in their regular column *PRYING INTO THE UNKNOWN*, related the following incredible story:

"It has always been a mystery to us in the first place how Mr. and Mrs. P.E. can find and afford the time to do the sort of things most of us only dream of doing. After knowing them for more than fifteen years, it is inconceivable to suspect their integrity or sanity - and yet they impose the following excise upon our credulity.

"While exploring for petroglyphs in the Casa Diablo vicinity of BISHOP, CALIFORNIA, Mr. & Mrs. P.E. came upon a circular hole in the ground, about nine feet in diameter, which exuded a sulphurous steam and seemed recently to have been filled with hot water. A few feet from the surface the shaft took a tangent course that looked easily accessible and, upon an impulse with which we cannot sympathize, the dauntless E.'s, armed only with a flashlight, forthwith crawled down into that hole.

"At a depth we've failed to record the oblique tunnel opened into a horizontal corridor whose dripping walls, now encrusted with minerals, could only have been carved by human hands, countless ages ago - of this the E.'s felt certain. The end of the short passage was blocked by what seemed to be a huge doorway of solid rock that, however, wouldn't yield. The light of their flash was turned to a corner where water dripped from a protuberance - which proved to be a delicately carved face, distorted now by the crystallized minerals, and from whose gaping mouth water issued.

"As Mr. and Mrs. E. stood there in silent awe - wondering what lay behind that immovable door - the strangest thing of all happened...but our chronology will not be incorrect if we wait till they return to the surface before revealing this, for now the water began gushing from the carved mouth and from other unseen ducts elsewhere in that cave and rising at an alarming rate!

"They hurried to the surface, and in less than half an hour there was only a quite ordinary appearing pool of warm mineral water on the desert floor.

"'Do you know,' Mrs. E. said to her husband, 'while I stood down there I heard music - the strangest, most weird music I'd ever heard. But it seemed to come from everywhere at once, or inside my own head. I guess it was just my imagination, but I can't really be sure.'

"Mr. E. turned pale. 'My God,' he said; I thought it was MY imagination, but I heard it, too - like music from some other world!'

"Why do they call that rock formation near where the E's had their strange experience Casa Diablo - the Devil's house? And why did the Indians name that area Inyo - dwelling place of the Great Spirit?"

Erich A. Aggen, Jr., in his article *TOP SECRET: ALIEN UFO BASES* (**SEARCH Magazine**, Summer 1991 issue), presented the following revelations concerning the UFO-subterranean connection: "...A great deal of UFO research has also led to the conclusion that various...species of aliens have set up secret underground bases in the United States and other countries. It is logical to assume that such bases have also been established elsewhere in the solar system. If such bases exist, where would we find them?

"EARTH BASES: UNDERGROUND - The dark, cavernous world beneath out feet is the source of many baffling mysteries. Clandestine UFO bases may be hidden deep within the earth in natural and/or artificial caverns. As a former member of the National Speleological Society (NSS), I am well aware of the vast extent of cave systems within the United States. In my own native state of Missouri, for example, there are over 2,500 known caves and dozens of new ones being discovered every year. Many of these caves are intricately linked together by numerous passageways and interconnecting chambers.

"One particular species of blind white (albino) cave fish, the TYPHLICHTHYS, has been found in many widely separated cave systems over several states. It has been found in caves that make a great arc through Kentucky, Indiana, Illinois and UNDER the Mississippi River extending into Missouri, Arkansas, and Oklahoma! A VAST SECTION OF THE CENTRAL AND SOUTHERN UNITED STATES MUST LIE ABOVE ONE IMMENSE CAVERN SYSTEM!

"Many caves possess rooms hundreds of feet in length, width, and height. In most cases, these huge natural caverns can only be reached and explored with the utmost skill and perseverance. There are only a few thousand NSS members in the United States and only a few hundred are active spelunkers. With so few spelunkers spread over such a large area, only a very small fraction of the tens of thousands of known caves in this country have been carefully mapped and explored. Thousands of other caves remain undiscovered and unexplored.

"Extensive evidence indicates that caves in the United States may be connected with caves in other parts of the world. In Mexico, the cave known as 'Sotano de las Golondrinas', (or) basement of the swallows, in the Municipio de Aquismo, S.L.P., reaches a depth of 1100 feet (334 meters). The cave is actually a giant 'sinkhole' or 'hole' in the ground with a nearly circular opening at the top, hundreds of feet in diameter. It is impossible to climb down the sides of Golondrinas because the walls of the opening are too smooth and "belled-out". To reach the bottom of the cave, a special rope over 1100 feet long must be secured at the top of the opening and dropped into the sinkhole. Explorers must then descend into the yawning hole one at a time using special cave repelling gear and climbing techniques. At the bottom of Sotano de las Golondrinas are numerous 'leads' or openings to a multiplicity of different crevices, passages, crawlways, and rooms that have never been mapped or investigated.

"The entrance to Golondrinas is located in one of the most primitive and uncivilized areas of Mexico and local inhabitants are afraid to approach the cave because they believe it is full of 'evil spirits' that lure people to their deaths. They tell stories of people mysteriously disappearing never to be heard from again while passing near the cave entrance. These stories may be based more on fact than fiction: they are similar in some respects to UFO abduction reports. Because of its huge size, remote location, and unique geological structure, Golondrinas would be an ideal UFO base. Naturally camouflaged caves in other parts of the world may serve as excellent natural bases, way stations, and 'depots' for UFOs.

"An underground nuclear test called the 'Schooner Experiment' conducted in December, 1968, substantiates the theory that caves in North and South America are intimately linked. In this test, a 35- kiloton nuclear bomb was exploded under the desert of Nevada. Five days after the test, the radiation level rose from 10 to 20 times in Canada, 1000 miles away from the Nevada test site! The only way the radioactive dust could have traveled that far is through an interconnected system of caves extending all the way from Nevada to Canada!"

Commander X's Guide to Incredible Conspiracies

Bourke Lee, in his book ***Death Valley Men*** (MacMillan Co.,N.Y. 1932), chapter: "Old Gold", describes a conversation which he had several years ago with a small group of Death valley residents. The conversation had eventually turned to the subject of Paihute Indian legends. At one point two of the men, Jack and Bill, described their experience with an 'underground city' which they claimed to have discovered after one of them had fallen through the bottom of an old mine shaft near Wingate Pass.

They found themselves in a natural underground cavern that they claimed to have followed about 20 miles north into the heart of the Panamint Mountains. To their amazement, they allegedly found themselves in an huge, ancient, underground cavern city. They claimed that they discovered within the city several perfectly preserved 'mummies', which wore thick arm bands, wielded gold spears, etc.

The city had apparently been abandoned for ages, except for the mummies, and the entire underground system looked very ancient. It was formerly lit, they found out by accident, by an ingenious system of lights fed by subterranean gases.

They claimed to have seen a large, polished "round table" which looked as if it may have been part of an ancient council chamber, giant statues of solid gold, stone vaults and "drawers" full of gold bars and gemstones of all kinds, heavy stone "wheelbarrows" which were perfectly balanced and scientifically-constructed so that a child could use them, huge stone doors which were almost perfectly balanced by counter-weights, and other incredible sights.

They also claimed to have followed the caverns upwards to a higher level which ultimately opened out onto the face of the Panamints, about half-way up the eastern slope, in the form of a few ancient tunnel-like quays. They realized that the valley below was once under water and they eventually came to the conclusion that the arched openings were ancient 'docks' for sea vessels. They could allegedly see Furnace Creek Ranch and Wash far below them.

They told Bourke Lee that they had brought some of the treasure out of the caverns and tried to set up a deal with certain people, including scientists associated with the Smithsonian Institute, in order to gain help to explore and publicize the city as one of the 'wonders of the world'. These efforts ended in disappointment however when a 'friend' of theirs stole the treasure (which was also the evidence) and they were scoffed at and rejected by the scientists when they went to show them the 'mine' entrance and could not find it.

A recent cloud burst, they claimed, had altered and rearranged the entire countryside and the landscape did not look like it had been before. When Lee last heard from the two men, Bill and Jack, they were preparing to climb the east face of the Panamints to locate the ancient tunnel openings or quays high up the side of the steep slope. Bourke Lee never did see or hear **from his friends ever again.**

In relation to the apparent connection between subterranean civilizations and unidentified flying objects, we will here quote from Paris Flammonde, author of ***THE AGE OF FLYING SAUCERS*** (Hawthorne Books, Inc., N.Y.), who tends to confirm this hypothesis.

He in turn quoted Raymond A. Palmer as a major proponent of this belief: "...The new decade was not without a new theory, or, at least, a variation of an old one, that not only were Flying Saucers not originating from beyond the farthest reaches of our planet, they were expelled from within it..."

Ray Palmer wrote a lengthy article elaborating his interesting and imaginative thesis, and prefaced it with the assertion that he was prepared 'to prove that flying saucers are native to planet earth; that the governments of more than one nation (if not all of them) know this to be the fact; that a concerted effort is being made to learn all about them, and to explore their native land; and that facts already known are considered so important that they are the world's top secret...' The continuation of his contention reads: '...is there any area on Earth which can be regarded as a possible origin for flying saucers? There are...four...the two major, in order of importance, are Antarctica and the Arctic...the two minor areas are South America's Motto Grosso and Asia's Tibetan Highlands.'"

Raymond Bernard (actual name 'Walter Seigmeister'), writing in the Oct. 1959 issue of **SEARCH** Magazine, p. 48, described yet another alleged encounter with a subterranean race. What are we to make of all these stories? Are we to assume that some of the individuals who told Bernard such accounts actually made them up, as some suggest, in order to receive the 'reward' Bernard was known to offer on documentable accounts of ancient tunnels? Or, are we to accept these accounts for just what their sources claim them to be, actual encounters with a subterranean world? Bernard stated the following:

"...Last week my investigators returned and said they visited their city (i.e. the 'city' of a race of dwarf-humans whom Bernard referred to as the 'Niebelungs', who live in a subterranean region with it's own system of illumination - Branton) and are able to bring any of my American friends to visit it, but I require one condition: absolute secrecy, as I don't want governments to send armies into the tunnel to disturb these peaceful people.

"To reach them requires a 3-day journey of about 40 miles through a tunnel. This entire distance is through a tunnel carefully lined with cut stone blocks below, above and on the sides. That was quite an engineering feat. I think the tunnel was made long to keep out curiosity seekers, and only the most determined will travel that distance.

"Here is the report of my investigations: (They are two ranchers, father and son, who discovered the tunnel accidentally):

"'We left our house 5 A.M. for the tunnel on top of a mountain and reached it 3 P.M. We were tired and camped near the entrance of the tunnel. For three days we proceeded through the tunnel. We told time by our watches, as we could not tell when it was day or night. We went to sleep at 10 P.M. and awoke at 3 A.M. and continued walking. By the third day the tunnel started to go downward by steps. It was built of stone blocks on all sides. By the night of the third day the tunnel suddenly opened into a great space covered with what appeared as a sky with a yellow light that made everything luminous, like daylight. We saw a city with many houses and saw many people in the distance. They were dwarfs with long white beards and long hair and we saw women and children, and heard them crying. The third member of our party got frightened so we had to return.' These men found three such tunnels. They entered another for three days, but after hearing voices further in, got scared and returned."

Branton is the author of **The Dulce Wars**, published by Global Communications.

Commander X's Guide to Incredible Conspiracies

PLANET X AND OTHER STRANGE EVENTS

Planet X is our Tenth Planet
By Mark Hazelwood

Planet X is our tenth planet, known from most historical records by many names. The average solar system is binary (has two suns) and has a dwarf that orbits back and forth or around the two suns. Our solar system is average in both regards. Pioneers 10 and 11 found our 10th(X) planet and our dark star twin sun and much effort has been made to keep this from the public.

The New Illustrated Science and Invention Encyclopedia Published by H.S. Stuttman Inc. Westport Connecticut 1987-89 Edition Clearly shown on the diagrams are our sun's dark twin Dead Star and Planet X, a.k.a. Niburu.

A dwarf is a label we've given to a celestial object that is a cross between a star and a planet. Our solar systems dwarf is sometimes referred to as Planet X. Its orbit around the two suns takes approximately 3600-3700 years to complete one cycle.

Much disinformation is being spread about Planet X. It's long orbit being unstable and thus not possible under the laws of physics is one of those lies. That statement would possibly be true if Planet X was orbiting just our one immediate sun instead of both suns. Disinformation is a combination of truth, lies, and omissions designed to keep the public in the dark. The omission of our solar system being binary and Planet X orbiting both suns is an attempt to stop the flow of this information from getting out to the public.

When Planet X enters our immediate solar system, its effects are far reaching, even at a distance. With it is close the sun regularly discharges major solar flares even during a solar minimum. Much extra electrical energy reaches earth as a result. Some of the earlier effects are unusual weather changes becoming normal, an up-tick in seismic and volcanic activity, melting of our poles, along with the overall ensuing environmental adaptations. These effects are typically things that are being blamed on particles from our dirty civilization or what is known as global warming. Global warming has all to do with our sun. Right now planet Mars is experiencing what we call global warming here and there are no SUV's being driven there.

The closer Planet X gets to our immediate solar system the more dramatic are its effects on it. Earth is not being singled out. It is believed that what we have termed Ice Ages, were in fact pole shifts. The gravitational pull upon our core, during its pass, can be great enough to dislodge our crust, resulting in a slip over the core. Someone described this as "the slipping peach skin effect". If you hold a peach in your hand long enough, apparently the skin will loosen and can then be slipped over the flesh of the fruit. It is believed that one of the poles from each planet will lock on to each other and in their dance, will create massive changes worldwide.

Censored books: ***Delicate Earth*** and ***Blindsided*** are not allowed to be sold in any major bookstore. This extremely serious subject is too hot to handle by the majority according to the powers-that-be. Lies, partial-truths, attacks, denials, attempts at making this subject appear humorous, and mainly silence are a small portion of the tactics being used to suppress this amazing knowledge. The evidence of Planet X and its IMMINENT PASSAGE, plus its entourage's continuing current passages FROM THE ONE SOUTHERLY DIRECTION and impacts on the sun are in the main the cause of:

Commander X's Guide to Incredible Conspiracies

1. The UNPRECEDENTED SOLAR ACTIVITY we are experiencing now in the middle of what should be the minimum part of the solar cycle. This is primarily due to the electromagnetic interaction with these objects.

2. So-called global warming which is all to do with the suns activity. Again, Mars is experiencing it too.

3. MAJOR CATASTROPHIC EARTH CHANGES that have accompanied previous passages, which is the MOST SIGNIFICANT ISSUE.

Since writing ***Blindsided*** the discerning eye brought forth about what to include in this work has become somewhat seasoned. Much revealing and clarifying information has come to light in the last three years.

Delicate Earth is the resulting historical chronicle of how the subject has progressed. Creating this book could be compared with producing a movie. The researchers, authors, insider disclosures, interviewers, and scientists are the stars of the book. Choosing and weaving their work together as an executive researcher/producer was in part my job as author, along with designing the cover, raising the money for printing and marketing. My writing is but a minor bit of the book.

The government disinformation-crew has helped me greatly in choosing to narrow my focus to the History and Science of Earth and Planet X. What the disinfo crew is most worried about they ignore or attack; namely the science, scientists, researchers, and history. What they offer on their web sites; prophesy, psychics, channeled aliens, outdated and bad science, I excluded. Now there will be no doubt about it. What people do with this knowledge is their business.

As many know there is a wide array of disinformation sites and people out there posing as individuals working to quash the Planet X awakening. It's a huge coordinated undertaking. These disinfo agents for the most part don't SEEM TO BE AFFILIATED WITH EACH OTHER. So, many disinformation sites and people attack each other to make it appear they are not working together.

I've named many people in this new work giving honest information. James McCanney's work is perhaps the best I've seen. In my new book ***Delicate Earth History Science Planet X***, I thank, cite, and name three pages of scientifically minded people who helped with the work; astronomers, physicists and astrophysicists, Nobel Prize winners, NASA scientists, professional and amateur investigators, military personnel, explorers, priests, scientific historians, investigative journalists, engineers, biologists, oceanographers, researchers, surveyors, astronauts, archeologists, geologists, anthropologists, and several authors of which many are doctors in their respected fields of research.

What is also addressed is the controversial relationship between the myriad of records from history, and ancient and modern science all relating to the effects of the cyclical passage of our tenth planet. Explore the cause of so-called Ice Ages in relationship to Polar Shifts believed to be the direct result of the electromagnetic gravitational interplay among the planets in our solar system. Learn of the Mastodons and Rhinos who were eating fresh tropical vegetation in Siberia, only 3650 years ago as well as the reason for their sudden dramatic death.

Find out about the reasons for our weather variations, drastically increased solar flare activity and why this largely negates commonly acknowledged so-called "Global Warming". Discover the connection between our Sun and the changes now taking place all over the world and understand why we can expect more dramatic effects. Father

Commander X's Guide to Incredible Conspiracies

Malachi Martin, eminent theologian, expert on the Catholic Church, served in Rome, where he was a close associate of the renowned Jesuit Cardinal Augustin Bea and Pope John XXIII.

This well respected triple doctorate stated on the Art Bell show in April of 1997, before his mysterious untimely death in 1999, that the Vatican has the larger part of the control of an observatory on Mount Graham in Arizona. When asked why the Vatican suddenly became interested in looking at deep space objects, his response was: "Because those at the higher levels, the highest levels of Vatican administration and geo-politics, have knowledge of what's going on in space, and what is approaching us, that could be of great importance in the next five to ten years."

The German magazine *Stimme des Glaubens*, has published the following account of Pope John Paul II's interview, with a small group of German Catholics, on the occasion of his visit to Fuida, in November of 1980. The question: "Holy Father, what has become of the 3rd Secret of Fatima? The Holy Father's response: "... it should be sufficient for all Christians to know this much: if there is a message in which it is said that the oceans will flood entire sections of the earth; that, from one moment to the other, millions of people will perish...there is no longer any point in really wanting to publish this secret message. Many want to know merely out of curiosity, or because of their taste for sensationalism, but they forget that 'to know' implies for them a responsibility. It is dangerous to want to satisfy one's curiosity only, if one is convinced that we can do nothing against a catastrophe that has been predicted."

In 1976 Zacharia Sitchin's groundbreaking book *The 12th Planet*, brought to life the ancient Sumerian's complete knowledge of our solar system. This included Niburu (Planet X), its' approximate 3600 year orbit, and the calamitous events expected during its' passage. Emmanuel Velikovsky, pioneer researcher in earth change catastrophism, author of *Worlds in Collision* and *Ages in Chaos* describes in detail what has happened to Earth before, and what is likely to happen in the future. In his book *Mankind in Amnesia*, he explains why those in power have intentionally erased past worldwide cataclysms from the collective consciousness of humankind. Authors John White - *Pole Shift* and Charles Hapgood - *Earth Shifting Crust*, have both picked up Velikovsky's trail and continue the research to reveal that geological data shows that the earth's crust has undergone repeated displacements.

Sufficient scientific and historical evidence exist, particularly from the application of plasma physics to the study of the solar system, to make it virtually inconceivable that there will not be major Earth changes again. The majority of us, through our cultural beliefs are expecting "something big". Many, sense on some level that we need to make changes in our lives. Some, who have learned of this celestial passage, or feel on some level that major earth changes are already happening, have begun to make physical survival preparations. As you delve deeper into this subject and connect this with other changes taking place in all of us, you will begin to perceive an extraordinary event unfolding.

Please see: www.planetxinbound.com
For Interviews, please contact Mark Hazlewood at 407 539-6563

Commander X's Guide to Incredible Conspiracies

The Role Of Disembodied Voices In The Overall Conspiracy
By Sean Casteel

Sean Casteel is a freelance journalist who has covered UFOs, alien abduction and other paranormal topics since 1989. He is also a contributing editor to *UFO Magazine* and is the author of *UFOs, Prophecy and the End of Time,* published by Inner Light Books. Visit his "UFO Journalist" website at: www.seancasteel.com

Do disembodied voices have a decidedly "vocal" say in how the overall conspiracy functions? Are top members of the government and military elite directed by a secret group of spirits of demonic origin? This is of course impossible to prove, as are most suspicions that are held about the New World Order and the many versions of how it operates. But it's at least worth a little conjecture.

According to psychiatrist Julian Jaynes, whose 1976 book *The Origin of Consciousness In The Breakdown Of The Bicameral Mind* is legendary among those who study the hard science behind many occult beliefs; mankind has heard voices since the beginning of creation. It is only in the last two millennia that their familiar sound has faded away to a whisper as mankind pressed on through the Age of Enlightenment and sought to prove "truth" with empirical reasoning alone.

Jaynes writes that in Biblical times, the most frequent contact with God was through a speaking voice heard directly in the mind. In fact, when a Hebrew was chosen out by the priest to be a prophet, the first step was to initiate him into a way of hearing voices. The implication, Jaynes argues, is that human experience of the nature of God is so bound up in the sound of a speaking voice that one can paraphrase the creation story in Genesis by saying, "In the beginning, the voices created the heavens and the earth."

Jaynes also outlines a concept he calls "The Authority of Sound," saying that the mere fact that a voice can make itself heard in a comprehensible manner automatically gives it a certain amount of authority over the listener. Whether the hearer believes what is being spoken to him or not, the physical nature of sound itself carries with it the ability to force both the listener's attention to and his understanding of what is being said.

Another researcher and author, Eric Norman, wrote an essential but relatively obscure book on the subject called Gods, Demons and UFOs. He explained that one of the early meanings of the word "demons" is "the knowing ones," primarily because they can both read a human being's mind as well as project a speaking voice into it that allows for a kind of "conversation" that takes place solely in the human brain. One of the most commonly reported torments suffered by mind control victims is again that of voices in the mind, voices that not only torture but seem to be quite consciously aware of the content of the mind control victim's thoughts.

So how does all this relate to the conspiracy? Again, according to Eric Norman, while disembodied voices today exist mostly in the realm of schizophrenia and other mental disorders, there has always been an elite group governing the world that has heard them. As an example, he talks about George Washington, Thomas Jefferson and the rest of America's Founding Fathers, all of who were Freemasons pledged to secrecy about the organization's practices. Norman says that at the very highest levels of Freemasonry, there is a disembodied voice phenomenon that directs the most highly placed members. He puts it very succinctly by saying, "There have always been voices at the top."

Meanwhile, the voice phenomenon has been slowly leaking to the general population. The 20th Century, Norman says, was a time drowned in "voices, voices, voices."

One complicating possibility could be that some of these voices hail from a different place in time, maybe even our own future. The Time Traveler Hypothesis that is often cited as an explanation for the UFO phenomenon could also apply to the voice phenomenon. How much easier it would be to project a simple speaking voice backward in time than to transport entire spacecraft along with their occupants. Perhaps some future mob, somehow "magically" empowered with the ability to scream through time, is looking back at this period and trying to warn itself in the past. The possibilities are endless.

But back to the political elite. If they are in fact subject to hearing voices, and those voices are demonic in nature, suddenly a great deal becomes clearer. For one thing, having our leaders subject to a phenomenon so decidedly identified with mental illness would ensure secrecy on the part of the conspirators. If no one admits to hearing voices, then those voices become impossible to prove, don't they? Any written records regarding them would surely be few in number and very classified.

Historically, these voices are known to chip away at the hearer's self-esteem in order to gain power over the human subject, as well as to inflate the hearer's ego with absurd delusions of grandeur as another method of control. Perhaps the second George Bush had been subject to exactly that form of demonic mistreatment, which resulted in a misguided war in Iraq. Both sides of the humiliation/aggrandizement coin may have combined to lead him to try to conquer feelings of weakness by an exercise in unneeded strength, going to war to salve a wounded ego.

Of course, all that could still be true without the presence of voices. Politicians could be rightly adjudged to be crazy without suffering the kind of symptoms that so-called "normal" people get put away for. But it is the purpose of this chapter to at least offer up the possibility that there is a form of order and of control being exercised over leaders in the government, the military, and the media that is so elusive because it can never be captured like a butterfly in a jar yet exerts a power over individual "players" that cannot be fought off with elementary human strategies. As is the case with schizophrenics, once you start hearing the voices, the real trick is to make them shut up.

Does Biblical prophecy deal with these voices? If you answered yes, you're right. The slow but inexorable spread of these voices into the general population could be what is meant when St. Paul writes in Second Thessalonians Chapter Two that the time of the Antichrist will not happen unless there be a "falling away" first. That falling away is also bound up in what Paul calls "the strong delusion," which the Lord himself sends to lead the wicked astray.

The idea of a "strong delusion," or a mass mental illness, would likely include the hearing of demonic voices that drive their hearers to the brink of madness and beyond. There is also a brief reference in the Book of Revelation to a "noisome pestilence," which could be another reference to mass mental illness caused by a noisy cacophony of voices.

There is of course a great deal more that could be said about this subject, but hopefully what is here will suffice to lay the groundwork for further exploration of the disembodied voice phenomenon. And if you should someday hear a voice projecting itself directly into your mind, you can at least tell yourself you're not the only one.

Commander X's Guide to Incredible Conspiracies

Things That Go Bump in the Night
By William C. Kern

At the risk of sounding like an escapee from a funny farm, I'll tell you about some weird things that have happened to me over the years. The first dream I can remember having was when I was only about 10 months old. I dreamed, in color, of seeing a man about 25 years old walking across a desert toward me. When he was a few yards from me he staggered and fell dead at my feet. But as he fell, I saw that the man was me.

A WORD OF EXPLANATION: Several people have written to question the statement that I was about 10 months old when I had a dream of myself as an adult and that I witnessed my own death. They thought I had made a mistake that I really meant 10 years old rather than 10 months old. No, folks, I really mean 10 months old. I have been haunted by the dream all my adult life. When I was in my early twenties, I described a house in Evansville, Indiana; the tall windows, the brick parking lot in back, the color of the house, the roof, the stairways, the location of the bedroom in which I slept, and the Maple trees lining the street outside the window, and asked my mother how old I was when we lived there.

She said I could not have been more than 10 or 11 months old because we had only lived in the house for a couple of weeks. I have never seen the house as an adult – indeed, have never even tried to find it. But I know exactly what it looked like inside and out back in 1937 when I was only 10 or 11 months old.

I was born dead, a result of breach birth, and considerable time and effort were expended to revive me. My mother told me I cried without cease for ten months, my anguish relieved only temporarily when she would hold me a certain way. But she said that I stopped the perpetual wailing when we moved away from the house and she has told me she believes that is when I received my "soul."

Having given that explanation to those who questioned it, I am now being told by some of them that I experienced a "walk-in." Mind you, others are making these claims, not I. I'm not sure I fully comprehend the "walk-in" event as explained by some of these people. If I understand what they're telling me, I was "taken over" by a discarnate human lifeform at age ten months (its consciousness waiting in limbo to inhabit my soulless earthly form) and that explains why I have heightened extrasensory perception (according to them).

Well, excuse me, but I'm unwilling to accept that idea. While I have no good explanation for the dream or why or how an infant could see himself as an adult or imagine his own death before he could even walk or talk, it would be easier to say I overheard someone talking or heard bits and pieces of a radio program while taking a nap and the ideas got implanted as a dream of myself.

As for the strong ESP; well, until recently I thought everyone was an esper to some degree. Maybe not. I cannot explain why I "see" events that are occurring hundreds or thousands of miles away, or events that have occurred within hours of my receiving the images. I've been able to "see" things all my life and, frankly, the power to do so has caused me a great deal of anguish, and I really don't like it much. If I had my druthers, I would prefer not to have the ability.

How could I describe the house inside and out right down to the brick car park in back at age 10 months? Well, just because I couldn't walk or talk doesn't mean that I was blind and stupid. I looked out the window; saw the environment, and my brain made a permanent recording. What's so hard about that? But whatever the truth of the matter is, I will need a lot more proof before I accept the notion that something "other" is living in my body.

The Dream Time

I had two recurring dreams from the time I was a baby until I was about 21 years old (already in the Navy, I served for 20 years). The first and most persistent dream was of an underwater world, a world of beautiful colors, swirling sea plants and some dangerous creatures.

People could "breathe" underwater, even I, although I often had trouble and was frightened. I would approach a large round basin or fountain on the surface of the planet, slip into it and swim downward into the underwater world. Sometimes I would stay for only a few minutes, sometimes for hours and hours (or so it seemed). I began having this dream at a very early age, perhaps one or two years old and it stayed with me until probably close to my 21st birthday (or the beginning of my fourth cycle of corporeal life). When I wrote this, I was 47 years alive. I am somewhat older now, having fallen to Earth to inhabit this fragile coil 67 years ago.

The other dream was of me and several other people hiding in a cave to keep from being eaten by a large cat. We would take turns poking the cat with a sharp pole when it tried to enter the narrow opening at the mouth of the cave. Over and over, year after year; it never got us and we never killed it. Same time frame: from about one year old until about 20 or 21 years old.

After 21 both dreams stopped and I've never had either of them again. Now...I am not certain I believe in reincarnation even if it might explain the dreams, the telepathy, the precognition and events like deja vu (which happens to me so often I don't even find it extraordinary anymore! I just go with it to see where it will lead).

During 1961 I was deployed to an African nation on a covert operation. While on this deployment, I was instructed to board an aircraft (Navy designation SNB; Air Force designation C-45) to fly to some unknown destination. The pilot, co-pilot and I were the only personnel on the plane. I recall taking off, looking out the window briefly at the Pacific Ocean on the left side of the plane, meaning that the plane was heading North toward Europe.

The next thing I can remember is standing beside a runway by myself watching a plane taking off. I believe the plane was a B-57. As the plane passed me, I knew it was not going to get airborne. It did not get off the ground but ran off the far end of the runway out of my sight. I remember turning away and thinking that I had correctly assessed the fate of the plane.

I cannot remember at which base I was when this event occurred. I think it may have been in Portugal or Spain, but it may have been in Italy, perhaps at a NATO base. I do have a hazy recollection of some sort of small green building near the edge of the runway where I went after the plane crashed. I also remember seeing a deHavilland Dragon Rapide aircraft parked there. I have no idea how I got there, what I did while I was there, or how I returned to the North African base where I was assigned on temporary duty.

The next thing I know is that I was performing my normal duties. This is not a case of a few missing minutes or hours, but my inability to recall an entire episode that may have taken a day or two, or weeks, and covered a distance of many hundreds of miles, and involved the crash of a United States military plane (perhaps with nuclear weapons aboard). A search of military aircraft accidents in one of those countries during that time might provide some information, if that information can be obtained; that is, if it is not still classified.

The Other Me?

When I was in Southeast Asia during the Vietnam conflict I was really in a dreadful state of mind; afraid of living and afraid of dying at the same time. I walked to the top of a hill where a chapel was located and I sat down on the lawn to look at the night sky. I was very sad and confused. I asked the "watchers" to give me some kind of message that would direct my life.

Suddenly I felt a warmth and peacefulness settling over me. I was completely at ease and calm. The pain in my heart went away. And another, older me from the future (or the past) appeared before me as an amorphous shape, and directed these exact words into my mind: "Every person is responsible for his own soul and none other," then vanished.

As simple as the words were, I understood every unspoken meaning! It was as though I was given, in that brief moment, the gift to see into my future and the meaning of endless life. It validated the substance and survival of the human soul, clarified my personal role as a manifest being, and verified life after death of the physical body. I was never afraid after that but I had many trials to endure before more meaning of the words were made clear.

At this same time I was working night shift at an intelligence agency. We worked 12 hours a day 12 days straight, then had one day off. One morning about 6:30 while I was examining some overflight reconnaissance film I suddenly "saw" a frightening image of a fan catching on fire at my home (which was several miles away) endangering my sleeping family. I was frantic! The image was as clear as if I were in the very room with the burning fan. I could smell the smoke; feel the heat of the flames! When the day shift came in to relieve us at 07:45, I rushed to my home to discover the fan wrapped in a charred blanket in the driveway. It had caught on fire exactly when I had seen it, but they had awakened in time to smother the fire and throw the fan onto the driveway!

During this same period of time, I watched two TLOs (Transient Luminous Objects) sailing over the military base for 45 minutes while standing the midnight to 0800 security watch. This sighting is detailed as follows:

In August 1968, I was standing the 2400 to 0800 security watch at a top-secret intelligence installation in Southeast Asia during the Vietnam conflict. I had just phoned the OOD at 0600 to report all secure and decided to step outside to get a breath of fresh air.

The two story concrete building was behind me. To my right was a range of low mountains obscuring approximately 20 degrees of the southern sky. To my left was (a bay) and the South China Sea. I was facing east where, about 20 miles away, another range of mountains obscured approximately 5 degrees of the sky.

Immediately after stepping outside the building I saw a bright luminous object gliding silently from west to east above the range of mountains on the right. I "felt" the presence of another object and turned toward the bay to see an identical object gliding at the same altitude and speed as the first. The objects were approximately one mile apart. The second object sighted made a sharp right turn, glided overhead at an altitude calculated to be 1200 to 1500 feet, passed behind the first object and disappeared from view beyond the mountain.

The first object sighted continued eastward at approximately 20 to 25 miles per hour. Both objects were as bright as a 1000-watt street light as seen from a distance of 200 feet. Neither object made any noise and neither object displayed any normal aircraft running lights. The objects were the size of a dime as seen at arm's length. I estimate their size to be 40 to 50 feet in diameter and spherical rather than elliptical in shape.

The first object was in sight for approximately 45 minutes. It did not deviate from its eastward course, nor did it pulsate or change colors. Its speed remained constant throughout the entire sighting.

I stood transfixed and was unaware that 45 minutes had passed until the morning crew began arriving for duty. At that time the eastbound object was a pinhead size bright light still visible on the face of the rising sun! I calculate that the object was approximately 20 to 25 miles away at the time I returned to the building.

I signed over the duty log, relinquished my sidearm and went back outside. The object was still visible on the lower edge of the rising sun that was approximately 10 to 12 degrees above the horizon.

I later remembered that the duty crash cameras, a 4x5 Speed Graphic and a 16mm Cine Special camera, were inside on the floor beside my chair and I had not even thought to take a picture!

I had been in the Navy for 12 years, the entire time as a photographer, a portion of that time as an aircrew member. My MOS was Photographer but my job was processing and printing overflight surveillance and intelligence film from U2s, RA3Bs, RF101s, RF4s, and other (at that time) secret reconnaissance aircraft. I had been around aircraft, both civilian and military, for fourteen years.

I cannot explain what I saw but I believe they were not fixed wing or rotary wing aircraft, not weather balloons (one turned, the other did not) and they were not celestial bodies or atmospheric phenomena.

My original assessment, although the objects appeared to be identical, was that I had seen two different things, one a weather balloon, the other a slow flying aircraft of some kind. Neither, however, displayed the movements or identification lights one would expect for either object.

Weather balloons, when blown by the wind (there was none that night) wobble and bob through the sky. Instrumentation packages swing below them, causing them to change shape and direction. Additionally, weather balloons are not lighted from within nor do the instrumentation packages carry such bright lights.

Helicopters can certainly fly at 20 to 25 miles per hour; however, none known at that time could fly silently at 1200 to 1500 feet. Neither of the TLOs emitted engine sounds or exhaust trails or displayed navigation lights.

When seen against the sun, even at a distance of approximately 25 miles, no hull shape or fuselage could be seen. The object seen against the sun appeared to have travelled in a straight line; that is, not following the curvature of the Earth. At last sighting, I estimate the altitude of the object to be 10,000 feet or higher above the ground.

Because of my background in photography and my experience as an aircrewman, I feel I properly calculated the altitude, speed and size of the objects. The description of the two TLOs does not fit any known aircraft or weather balloon. They do, however, perfectly define the phenomena known as Transient Luminous Objects that have been shown to glide silently and slowly for long distances, change directions with apparently intelligent purpose and emit no sounds or exhaust trails.

TLOs do not display any signs of hostility or covert curiosity. They do not damage objects or affect the environment in any apparent manner. They simply appear, move about the skies for a time, then glide away or vanish; leaving stunned and confused witnesses to wonder what they have observed.

Unlike the objects known as UFOs, which seem to have destinations and purpose, and are solid and three-dimensional (or more), TLOs are truly unexplainable phenomena having no observable substance or core, no common size or brightness, no common speed or direction. They may forever remain a mystery to those of us who have been fortunate enough to see them.

Enlightened

A couple of years later, back in the States and working on the space programs, I one day fell into a kind of trance or state of stasis or suspended animation. All sound and feeling and normal senses disappeared. I was awake but could not move. I wasn't afraid or worried. My thoughts were never more clear and attuned. From the ceiling (passing through the ceiling from outside the building, it seemed to me) a very bright orb of light (TLO?) appeared and floated down to cover me. I could hear sounds that might have been voices but were not in a language I could understand.

I remember a low-pitch music-like tone, very soft and pleasant. I was wrapped in the light and sound for what seemed to be 10 or 15 seconds, then the light floated up through the ceiling, leaving me wondering what had happened! Almost two hours had passed while I was "in the light."

A couple of years later on March 27, 1977, I was painting a house in El Centro, a dusty border town in southern California when suddenly I "saw" an island and the crash of two large airplanes. They exploded on the ground. One plane taking off collided with another crossing its path. Many hundreds of people were killed in the fire. I was shaken and horrified! It was as though I was suspended in the air above the airport watching it.

I put the brush and paint away and went into the house to call my mother because I thought something had happened to my family. The television was on. As I was dialing the number in Indiana, the announcer said (paraphrase), "We interrupt this program to bring you this special news bulletin. Two 747 Jumbo jets have collided at Tenerife Airport in the Canary Islands. Officials fear many hundreds are dead, most burned to death in the fire following the crash."

575 people died in that crash, most within just a few minutes. I was very shaken by that experience for a long time. I don't know what these events mean. I'm not particularly seeing an event that I can change or stop; I am either seeing the event as it occurs or shortly after or before it occurs. What does that mean? I don't know, but it sure has caused me a lot of pain and sadness for many years. Prior to this I had "seen" a figure standing near me or watching me from a short distance away, but only from the "corner of my eye." If I looked directly at the figure I couldn't see it. But in 1974 or 75 I saw the figure fairly clearly sometime after the light came from the ceiling to cover me.

I know this sounds insane but the figure appeared to be a male dressed in an ornate costume I would guess to be Eastern Indian (Hindu). His skin was brown and he was slightly built, trim but strong looking. Never said a word; just followed me around. No one else saw him because no one else ever looked at him or said anything about him.

I used to think of this person as a guide or "watcher." As my life grew more complex and hectic after I retired from the Navy, I never saw the guide again. I was working long hours without eating or sleeping and my life went to pieces. Pretty soon I was getting divorced and ended up living in my truck as a homeless person for almost three years.

It was during this time that I saw an extremely bright TLO descend from the night sky east of El Centro, California and sail toward Anza in the Northwest at an apparent altitude of about 3000 feet.

Discarnate Spirit

After I married Jane, we traveled around the US for almost a year, and then came back to San Diego to settle down. We bought a mobile home and moved in; learning soon afterwards that a lady had died in the house not long before we bought it.

Well, I used to see the woman standing at the end of the hallway watching me tear up her house (remodeling). She walked back and forth, back and forth, the floor creaking and groaning as she passed. Sometimes she would push the dishes from the counters into the sink. Sometimes she would open and close the doors. Eleven years later she still walked the halls, opening and closing doors, pushing papers, magazines and other objects to the floor at all hours of the day and night. (In 1996 these events ceased.)

I have seen solid objects and lights in the skies since I was a very small child. Once I was walking through a field far from my home. I was two or three years old. Suddenly I saw an object streaking from the sky directly at me. It entered my chest and knocked me to the ground. I felt no pain (that I can recall) and remember thinking, "Why have they done this to me?" I was sad that the white object had hit me and knocked me down. I felt as if I had been punished for something.

I got up and went home. A few minutes after I returned home I heard sirens (I didn't know what "sirens" were then and I was very frightened by the sound). I fell onto my bed, crying and my mother had to comfort me.

A large old barn at the end of the field had been set on fire by some vandals and was destroyed. I had been heading straight for that barn when the object came from the sky and knocked me to the ground!

Now, I ask you, what was that?

"I was certain if I willed it strongly enough, I would eventually fall upward into the sky."

During the Second War, when I was about five years old, my dad had a small boat upturned over two saw horses in the back yard of our home in Evansville, Indiana. I used to climb onto the boat and jump off, sometimes for hours on end, certain if I willed it strongly enough, I would eventually overcome gravity and fall upward into the sky. It is just as well that I didn't because I had made no plans to get back down to the ground.

Once, after landing hard and rolling over on my back, I saw a grey colored spindle-shaped object hovering in the sky directly above me. It made no sounds. I watched it for a short period of time then returned to my goal of learning to fly.

When I was 11 or 12 years old I saw another odd and very large object hovering low in the sky to the east of our farm home in Washington, Indiana. I watched the object for about 30 minutes through a pair of binoculars. It remained fixed in the sky although the clouds were scudding quickly to the east. It made no sounds.

In 1968 I saw three silver objects speed from south to north above San Diego, California at an altitude of 30,000 to 50,000 feet. Seen from near the Mexican border they were out of sight in about three or four seconds. They made no sounds.

Things in the Room

Recently, while sitting here writing one of my reports, I heard a voice as clearly as I can hear Jane when she walks into the room, saying, "What do you think you're doing?" I nearly jumped out of my skin for certain! I was so frightened by the voice that I got up and left the room for the rest of the day. It wasn't Jane because she was in the back bedroom. It was just a voice from behind me and to the right, about a foot from my ear.

Sometimes I feel as if people or things are touching me. Could be a muscle twitch, I don't know. Fairly well unnerves me, truth to tell! Sometimes I hear sounds like a recorder playing fast forward, people talking very fast! I look but nothing is there.

Postcognitive Dream

I had disturbing, confused dreams on the 2nd of February 1993, about my firstborn child, Cindy, then 36 years old and working at WRNO Radio in Metairie, Louisiana. In the dream we were walking together through narrow, dark streets. Tall buildings were on both sides. A few people were still out and about. We were looking for something but neither of us knew what it was. Eventually we became separated and I began looking for her. I could hear her calling, almost frantically, as I ran down the dark streets.

At one point I thought I saw her in the distance so I began running toward her. I stumbled over something on the sidewalk and looked down. There, bundled into a hand-quilted comforter, was a body. It was completely covered, so I didn't know who it was.

As soon as I looked up, I was standing beside my daughter and we began to make our way home. I'm not certain we ever made it because I forced myself to wake up.

During breakfast, I was so distracted by the dream that I told Jane about it. After breakfast, I began working but I just couldn't get the dream out of my mind. I felt a terrible fear and overpowering sense of dread. Finally, unable to concentrate, I made a call only to find that Cindy's mother was on her way to Indiana because her mother (my ex-mother-in-law) had died over the weekend!

She used to make hand-sewn comforters!

Cindy had moved to Metairie only a week before and I didn't know her address or phone number so I couldn't call. I didn't have to. Shortly after noon, Cindy called me to tell me the bad news. When I told her I already knew she wasn't even surprised. But she told me she had been crying all night and was very sad and lonely, had been unable to sleep and had sat up in bed until 4 am wishing someone could be there with her.

"But, Cindy," I said, "I was with you last night." And I told her all about the dream. Well, Cindy needed to talk, so I mostly listened for about two hours until she got it all out then began telling me about New Orleans and the shops and the magic and the Mississippi River and how much she loved it and how great her job was.

I suspect I needed to hear her talking about as much as she needed to talk, so it was no surprise that a couple of hours went by before she finally decided it was time for her to get ready to go to work. By the time we hung up our phones, we were both okay, which just goes to show that if we are willing to keep the channels open, all kinds of things find their way into our minds, including love and caring and sharing, and long-distance cries for help.

And, yes, I called Indiana for the first time in about eight years and offered my sympathy to the family. When asked how I knew of their mother's death, I told the story of the nightmare and the feelings of fear and dread like something horrible had happened.

The daughter asked, "Oh? Can you still see things?"

Yes, I can still see things. Can't everyone?

Actually, I wouldn't try to analyze this event if someone paid me. I had a strange dream with a dead person and my frightened daughter in it. A couple of telephone calls explained it as far as I can tell.

Things like this happen to me so often that I would be surprised if something occurred in my family that I couldn't "see." I'd feel like I wasn't paying attention or something!

Once I had a dream that I was flying in an airplane with a friend and the plane passed over a house on the final approach. Some people were in the yard looking up with their hands shading their eyes from the bright sky. The plane crashed when it landed and we were both killed. I woke up and was alive. Whew.

Later that morning the friend called and asked me if I wanted to go flying! This is the truth: I absolutely did not know he had a pilot's license! I said okay, even though I remembered the dream. I figured it was a coincidence. About an hour later we were up having a good time. We flew around a bit and looked at the scenery then he decided to practice some touch and goes. Over the highway and turn toward the field. Down below is a house. People are in the yard. They look up, protecting their eyes from the bright sky, just as I saw it in my dream a few hours earlier. My heart goes pitty-pat! But I changed the future. In the dream I was terrified when I saw the people because I already knew that they knew we were going to crash. I relaxed. I had nothing to fear.

"Every person is responsible for his own soul and none other."

I even smiled, perfectly content and unafraid. My friend made a very poor landing, about as close to a crash-landing as he could make without tearing that airplane to pieces, but we didn't get hurt. Needless to say, I never went flying with him again.

Another on 9/11

I wonder how many people can relate to this one. On the evening of September 10th, 2001, Jane and I stopped at a KOA park in Alatchua, Florida. Sometime in the early morning hours of the 11th, I had an extremely vivid dream of large airplanes flying into the United Nations building in New York and the Capitol building in Washington, D.C. Right cities, wrong buildings.

The dream was so vivid and real, that I awoke and was unable to go back to sleep. At daybreak, we unhooked the motor home and continued on to Ocala. When we arrived there, my brother, who was also visiting our mom, came out to tell me that two planes had crashed into the towers.

I put my hands to my face and cried out, "My God, I had a dream about it last night!"

Their son-in-law, who worked for the Port Authority and whose office was in one of the towers, was late for work that morning by about 15 minutes.

We all know the rest of that story.

There's More, But...

Okay, those are some of my odd stories. The precognition or telepathy and the translocation has really bothered me all my life because I sometimes suspect I have caused these events to happen by thinking them first. In other words, I'm not seeing something that is happening but I am thinking something and making it happen! I try to tell myself that I couldn't do that, that I'm not capable of killing 575 people no matter where they are, but I'm not sure of that, see? Who knows what might have happened to me while I was working in the intelligence community? Who knows but that we might slip into alternate reality of time and space while we sleep?

But you see, my precognition doesn't help anyone (maybe once it helped me since I saw a way to change the outcome of a bad landing) and I don't seem to be able to stop terrible things from happening. It is more like I am in tune with events near the time they happen. No matter what I do, they still happen. People still die and I still worry that I have made it happen by dreaming it or "imaging" it.

In 1986 I wrote a novel, *The Morningstar Conspiracy*, the plot of which was an engine, called a "Cascade Generator," developed to drive spacecraft and machines of the next century. The military planned to use it for secret excursions into space and for driving conventional weapons of war.

Had the engine been introduced to the market, it would have destroyed civilization by eliminating half the jobs in the world, jobs which are based upon a fossil fuel economy. It was up to the hero and heroine, with some help from an intelligence agent, to see that did not happen.

I am convinced this engine exists, whether it is being used as I suggested or not. In March 1993 I learned that an engine, identical in size, design and even name had been designed in 1930, six years before I was born, and had been purchased by the company that is now Mobil Oil for exactly the reasons stated in my book!

I had never heard of the engine or of the inventor or the name, "Cascade Generator." Where did those thoughts and ideas come from? How could I have imagined a duplicate engine of the same size with the same purpose and with the same name unless I had somehow received thoughts from someone during the period when I was living alone as a homeless person in my truck (which is when I conjured up the idea for the book)? The book was published in 1988.

So many things happened in the Navy that should have killed me but passed over my head or around me that I cannot number! I was on the flight deck crew of an aircraft carrier, the most dangerous place in the world! Planes crashed, fires raged, tractors almost ran over me, pieces flew in all directions. Through my entire Navy career people were injured and even killed, but I got not a scratch. I was snatched out of the way at the last minute or saw flying, burning, falling pieces batted away before they hit me.

Well, there are more events that would take months to write about, but you get the idea, I think. I suspect I have lived several times before this and that worries me no end.

What I want to know is - WHY! Why would a person remember things from another life, like walking across a desert in a silver costume and dropping dead at his own feet? Even if we do live more than one life, why do we, how do we, remember events that may have occurred centuries before our present manifestation of Earthly flesh, or, indeed, may have occurred on another planet in another space, in another time?

How or why could I see me talking to myself in front of a church one night in Southeast Asia and knowing from the words that the universe is a great deal more than it appears to be? Why was I covered with a bright light for a few seconds that turned out to be two hours and then see a figure following me around for several years?

What was the message in seeing several naked people trying to keep a large cat from eating them in a cave? Why did I "dream" I was floating in a surreal underwater world over and over for almost 20 years? And why did something streak from the sky and knock me to the ground to prevent me at two years old from going into a barn that was about to be set on fire?

Why do I remember chums and events from a childhood that I have never experienced in this lifetime; in particular, swimming in an abandoned stone quarry with dozens of other children, a quarry that I know I have never seen or visited in this life. What am I supposed to do with this information? If I am here to accomplish something, what is it and when will I receive the final instructions? Have I already received them? Am I receiving them on a daily basis, little by little? I welcome your comments. Oh, a visit to a sanitarium has already been suggested, so please don't.

Commander X's Guide to Incredible Conspiracies

ANOMALOUS BEINGS, REPTILIANS AND SHAPE SHIFTERS

Reptilians at Montauk
By Michelle A. Guerin

On the southeastern most tip of Long Island, lays the idyllic fishing hamlet of Montauk, NY. Quiet and sparsely inhabited during the cold, wind-strafed months of winter, the town's population swells each summer with the onslaught of tourists, fishermen and those fortunate to have season residence in this quaint seaside village. Many "day" visitors flock to see the historic landmark, the Montauk Lighthouse, commissioned by the "Father of Our Country", George Washington.

But there is a darker side of Montauk Point that many are unaware of. Within view of the famous lighthouse lies a derelict military facility, known as Camp Hero. A Sage Radar dish sits atop a tall, abandoned building in the distance. Records show Camp Hero was officially decommissioned and vacated by the US Air Force in 1969. It was reopened and operated without the sanction of the US Government, utilizing a fully verified and documented subterranean facility beneath the base. And it is here, many believe, the Montauk Project was able to carry on its covert operations.

What Is The Montauk Project?

According to Preston Nichols and Peter Moon, authors of ***The Montauk Project: Experiments In Time***, the Montauk Project "was a development and culmination of the phenomena encountered aboard the USS Eldridge in 1943." This is popularly known as the Philadelphia Experiment, a series of experiments conducted by the U.S. Navy involving radar invisibility.

"According to these accounts," states Peter Moon, "over three decades of secret research and applied technology ensued. Experiments were conducted that included electronic mind surveillance and the control of distinct populations. The climax of this work was reached at Montauk Point in 1983. It was at this point that the Montauk Project effectively ripped open a hole in space-time to 1943."

Allegations have been made of ongoing research and experimentation into psychotronics, electromagnetic mind control and the manipulation of space and time to allow for the successful transport of matter and energy into other dimensions through "portals" or time warps. These projects are reportedly being carried out by the combined efforts of clandestine units of the CIA, NSA, DARPA and other government agencies, military intelligence and corporations with strong defense-related ties.

Allegedly, a particle accelerator is being used for powering particle beam weapons and radar systems, as well as HAARP-like transmissions of high- powered radio frequencies into the ionosphere. There is purported evidence of additional particle accelerators at nearby locations. Brookhaven National Labs, a research facility on Plum Island, and a military facility at West Hampton Beach, have been mentioned as possible sites.

I have attempted to chronicle the numerous incidents, and subsequent research and investigations that indicate my apparent personal involvement with the Montauk Project. The investigation is far from complete...for it appears the deeper we go, the more we unearth. I have determined it is more important to alert others of the REALITY of the Montauk Project and, in doing so, garner the assistance necessary to pursue the truth. While some details may seem innocuous, I include them in the event future verification is needed.

The Sands Of Time

It was mid-September, 1994. It had been almost 25 years since I had visited Montauk, NY. As I stepped off the train, I wondered still, why I felt the need to go there. I was trying to come to terms with and reach some understanding of my apparent involvement with alien abductions. I was seeing Dr.Maurice Kouguell, PhD., a clinical psychologist specializing in hypnotherapy, to assist me in overcoming anxiety caused by these experiences.

At Montauk, the busy summer season had ended, and I looked forward to relaxing, doing some reading on the subject of alien abductions, and with any luck, finding some answers. I spent 4 days at Montauk. With each passing day, I got more and more depressed. I did not venture any further than a few blocks in either direction of my hotel. I couldn't wait to leave and returned home on Friday.

The next night, after falling asleep around midnight, I was abruptly awakened by the violent vibrating of my bed and my body. It felt as though an earthquake had hit me. However, I suddenly sensed I was not alone. I was unable to see anything. I don't know if my eyes were open or not, but I could feel my body being pulled from the bed.

I still remember how the sheet felt as my body was pulled across it. I tried to scream "Oh God", but it came out as a whisper. I screamed in my head: "No...I'm still awake". By this time, my hips were at the edge of the bed. I turned and tried to grab for the headboard, to drag myself back. That was the last thing I remembered before losing consciousness.

The next morning I remembered none of this. Later that evening, while talking to a friend on the phone, it suddenly came flooding back to me. I quickly finished the conversation, too upset to talk, and changed for bed. That's when I first noticed the 2 puncture marks on my left thigh. They were about 2 inches apart...midway between my knee and the top of my thigh.

I was determined to have a record of this latest physical manifestation of my experiences. At the time, I worked for Dr.D, an internist. I asked him to please look at these marks and to tell me if they were indeed puncture marks. He examined them and stated that they "appeared to be puncture marks", but they were "too symmetrical" and "how could I get them and not know how it happened?"

I decided it was time to tell him how it happened. After hearing my story, he recommended I see a psychiatrist. I made an appointment with a local doctor. I spent close to an hour telling Dr.S of my experiences. When I was finished, he advised me that he did not believe in the possibility that life existed elsewhere in the universe. I said that he was going to tell me I was suffering from night terrors and sleep paralysis. He concurred with that diagnosis. I asked him how it was possible to have puncture marks associated with this diagnosis. He had no answer. I then asked him if I was neurotic, psychotic or suffering from delusions. He said no. I stated, "Well maybe, just maybe, I am telling you the truth". Before I left his office, I told him at this point the best we could say, is that we had agreed to disagree. And I hoped we could have this conversation again

10 years from now. I eventually saw Dr.Kouguell concerning this episode. The puncture marks were still visible and I showed them to him.

Prior to this experience, I had related to Dr. Kouguell partial accounts of my encounters with a species I referred to as "the nasty ones". Even after regression, I was unable to get a clear image in my mind of their appearance. All I could draw was a picture that resembled a "fat plant leaf ". I also had a strange response to a silhouette image, and subsequent flash image, of an alien depicted in an episode of the *X-Files*. I was terrified. The image was of a large, muscular being with pronounced, pointed ears.

While attending a UFO conference in New Jersey in March of 1995, I arrived late to a lecture and slide show being presented by Leah Haley. The slide show was already in progress when I took my seat. After just a few minutes, an image appeared on the screen that caused me to panic and become so anxious, I had to leave the room. The image she had drawn was of a reptilian being she had encountered during an abduction. It showed the same pointy ears I had seen on the *X-Files* episode. Later, I was to realize this is what I had drawn for Dr. Kouguell. The image of the "fat plant leaf " was the distinct shape of the alien's ears.

I had started to hear about a covert operation called the Montauk Project. I became very interested in learning more about it since I lived so close to Montauk. I read the 3 books written by Preston Nichols and had very uneasy feelings about this story. Why was I drawn to this place? Why did I feel the need to learn everything I could? In one of the books is a picture of Duncan Cameron. The face was so familiar to me...I knew I had had a conversation with him at some time and then realized it had been telepathic! But I could not remember what the conversation had been about, or when it had occurred.

Louise, a friend, and I were planning to attend a UFO conference in CT in October 1995. I suggested that since she was driving up to NY to pick me up for the conference, why not come a few days early and we would explore at Montauk. She immediately agreed.

Upon arriving in Montauk, we checked in to our hotel room, and set off for Camp Hero. We tried different entrance points but all had security gates and signs posted stating no trespassing. We finally found access on a side road just before the Lighthouse. It was an area just south of the base, on the beach. The road we walked on ended at a parking area on a cliff overlooking the ocean. The radar dish was visible from this point, but was too far to hike to.

Louise felt very sick and uneasy there. For some reason, I was drawn to the cliff. I stood out there by the edge, just looking out over the beach and the ocean for about 10 minutes. I felt so drawn to this spot...why? What possible reason could there be? I had never been there before. Why did I feel rooted to the spot? It was getting late and Louise and I wanted to try one more road before we called it a day.

Driving back toward the town, we turned in at Old Montauk Highway. According to the map we had, this road should go into Camp Hero. There was also notations on the map of areas where someone had "felt a void" and very ominous feelings.

While driving down the road, Louise and I both felt this "void". It was one of the strangest feelings I've ever felt. The only way I can describe it is the absence of feeling life, as if nothing lived in this space. I wish I could be more specific. Once past this void, the terrible, ominous feeling hit us very strongly. The road ended abruptly at a dead end. Louise wanted to go back to the hotel, but I insisted that I knew we were close to the radar dish and wanted to check around just a little.

Commander X's Guide to Incredible Conspiracies

I climbed over a pile of wood chips and went through some small brush. About a hundred feet into the brush the asphalt road continued. I followed it to a clearing and there it was, right in front of me...the radar dish. I went back to the car, where Louise was waiting and grabbed the video camera. I returned the same way, taping as I went along. After shooting the radar dish, I suddenly got an eerie feeling that I was being watched. The feeling was very strong and very frightening. I wanted to run back to the car, but I was afraid I would fall. I left as quickly as I could. Louise and I returned to the hotel.

We went to bed about midnight but I stayed up until approximately 1:30am reading. Sometime between 3:00 - 3:30am both of us were awakened by a loud noise. The smoke detector in our hotel room was going off and neither of us could reach it in order to turn it off. We finally contacted a hotel employee who advised us that the smoke detector was not run off a battery, it was connected directly to the room's electrical system. In order to shut it down, we should go to the fuse box located on the side of the closet wall and throw the switches until we found the one connected to it. We tried all of the switches to no avail. Even throwing the main switch, which cut power off to the entire room, did not shut down the smoke detector. A maintenance employee of the hotel came to our room and tried shutting down the electricity...the detector still continued. He finally had to pull the smoke detector from the wall and cut the wires in order to turn it off. The next day, we agreed that neither of us wanted to return to the base. We were both too frightened.

A couple of weeks later, I was scheduled to attend a UFO conference in Mobile AL. I went down a few days early to get away by myself a little. It was during this time that the flashbacks started. First, the face of the reptilian, close to mine, accompanied by a rasping sound. I knew the reptilian image was during my...rape? But when – where? I didn't have the answers. Then I saw an image of travelling in a military jeep, through tall grass and sand, over hills, soldiers wearing fatigues (brown/tan/black) and black berets. I had also recalled a memory of being submerged in some type of fluid...heavier than water. I kept hearing muffled sounds of people talking and remembered yelling, "I can't hear you." These flashbacks continued to haunt me, but I couldn't remember any other details.

It was during the period after my return from Mobile that I remembered a strange experience in Montauk in 1970. When questioned about periods of "missing time", I had always stated that I didn't have any. But I suddenly remembered that I had! For whatever reason, I had no recall of it until this time. During a visit to my aunt and uncle's campsite at Ditch Plains in Montauk, I was missing for 2-3 hours and my uncle remembered it! My recollection of the early part of that day had always been very clear. My memory of the later part of the day had always been vague and blurry.

I had an appointment with Dr.Kouguell that week and determined I should regress to that day in 1970 to see what really happened. I told Dr.Kouguell that I felt he should put me under as deeply as he could...he agreed.

The following text is my recollections while under hypnosis: 11/9/95 Session. We are driving in the car, on our way to Montauk. I'm sitting in the front seat with my mom. My brothers and sister are in the back seat. Daddy is at work. Mom is so happy we're going to Montauk. Uncle B is her half-brother...they just met a couple of years ago, at the funeral of her natural father. We arrive at Ditch Plains, the campsite they stay at in Montauk. I hang around for a little while, talking with everyone, then decide to change into my bathing suit (a two-piece) but put my cutoffs on over my bathing suit bottom.

Commander X's Guide to Incredible Conspiracies

This is so boring. I'm going to look around the campsite.

I walk towards the east a little way and after awhile I pass by a group of surfers camping there. One of them looks familiar...it's M! F's older brother! I stop to say hello. M asks me if I've seen F yet, I tell him no. He says F is surfing right now, so I decide to walk down to the water and look for him. I sit on the sand at the shoreline, watching 5-6 surfers. Finally, I spot F. He is so beautiful! When he heads in from the water, I get up and start walking in his direction. I hope he notices me. As I get closer, he does. He calls out my name and waves. I walk over and we kiss hello. He asks what I'm doing in Montauk and I tell him. He asks if I'd like to take a walk in about an hour. He's got some things he has to do back at the campsite, can I meet him there? Sounds GREAT!

This hour is going so slow. I'm at the campsite with F and we start walking towards the east. We walk a little less than a mile. There's a cliff up ahead and we walk into the dunes to find a quiet spot. There's tall dune grass behind us. F's got a towel, so we sit down on that and start making- out. We end up lying down next to each other. He kisses so well.

Suddenly, I hear a loud buzzing sound, like a lot of bees. I sit up and so does F. What is this? Something's not right! I look at F and he can hear it too. We lay down on our backs, still next to each other. Why am I doing this? We should run away! I try to yell to F that we should get out of there. But I can't talk...I can't move! I'm so scared...I want my mother!

It sounds like a car is coming...the sound gets closer, then stops. The buzzing is louder now. Even though I'm scared, my body acts like it's not. A man wearing a soldier uniform is looking down at me, standing on my left. On the right, is another soldier; he kicks F's leg. "He's out of it", he says. "Mike, you take him to the jeep" says the leader on my left. "Ok, Terry", says the guy on my right. There are two other guys with them, but I don't know their names. Terry is very tan, with dark hair and dark glasses. The others seem to be fairer. Mike and another guy pick up F and Mike carries him like the firemen do. Terry doesn't pick me up someone else does.

We're in the back seat of a jeep, traveling north, through the dunes and tall grass. There's a big hill up ahead. This is so weird! The hill is moving...just part of it. It looks like a door in the hill. It moves forward and then to my right. We drive in. There is another jeep parked on my left. Two other men in the same uniform with the black beret are inside. They all have rifles! I still can't talk, but my body does what they want. I'm helped from the jeep. F is between two guys and they are helping him walk. Terry and someone take me between them and I can walk, too. This place looks like a garage or something. We go through a door. It's bright in this hallway. We turn right. F is just ahead of me. At the next hallway, F keeps going straight with two guys, but we turn to the right and walk a few feet to an elevator door. Terry has a credit card and puts it in a slot next to the door. The slot is vertical and there are two lights above it...one red, one green.

The door opens and we go inside, but there are no buttons to push. We're going down, then door opens and it's much darker here. And it smells funny...like a basement with a cesspool overflow problem. We turn right and go a few feet...then turn left. I'm so cold! There's a door on my left – Terry opens it. This room is so dark I can hardly see. There's almost no furniture in it. There's something that looks like a padded table. They help me on it and lay me down. Now I'm really cold.

One guy says, "Do we just leave her here?", and Terry answers, "she's not going anywhere". They leave the room. I can't seem to move anything but my eyes. Why am I here? I don't like this. Over to my left, something moves. It's coming closer...I can see it better. OH MY GOD! It's a monster!

(Note: At this point I got so agitated and almost jumped from the recliner in Dr. K's office. My eyes flew open and I couldn't stop shaking and cringing. Dr. K calmed me down and I could continue.)

What I see is a creature about 6-7 ft tall. His ears are large and pointed at the top. His eyes are bright yellow-gold and seem to glow. He has pointy teeth and a large wrinkle on his forehead and he has a TAIL! He's coming towards me...I have never been so scared in my life. He comes to the foot of the table. He pulls off my shorts and bathing suit bottom...he pushes my legs open and pulls me down towards him. His face is so close to mine...I want to scream, but it's only in my head. I hear a raspy sound coming from him. He puts something inside me and I feel like I'm being ripped apart. He likes to see how terrified I am...it gives him a lot of pleasure. It hurts so much. I have to get away in my head to someplace safe. I go.

I don't know how long he does this, but when he is done, he goes back to the part of the room I first saw him in and then he is suddenly gone. The door never opens or anything; I don't know how long I lay here. Terry and another guy come through the door and dress me. They help me from the table and we leave the room. After I am brought back up the elevator, I am taken into another well-lit room. It reminds me of a doctor's examining room...except there are machines I don't recognize with lights and dials recessed in the wall above a counter area. There is a lot of stainless steel equipment. And a table covered in white. I am placed on that table and strapped down...including my head. I am terrified. I am left alone for what probably is just a few minutes...but it seems like hours.

A group of five or six people comes into the room. They are wearing white gowns and masks and hats that covered their heads. They are male, but I see at least one female. They are very busy. I don't know why.

My head is turned on its side and taped to the table. I know this sounds strange, but a small portion of the area above and behind my right ear is shaved. My ear is pulled toward the front of my face and taped to it! Although I am immobilized and can't talk I am completely conscious!

Someone is writing something on the skin behind my ear. I remember someone is saying something about an "IV". And a man says, "Do you think she need's it?" Someone else says, "I wouldn't want to take a chance that she might wake up and start moving around". A few minutes later I feel a prick in my arm.

That's all I remember until I regained consciousness back on the dunes with F. *Note: About 10 years ago, I developed what was thought to be an inflamed cyst behind my right ear. The doctor had to lance it to drain and remove it. As he broke the skin with the scalpel, something shot out. He examined it and said he had never seen anything like it. He said it was the size and shape of a bullet. He had to pack the hole it left with medicated gauze.

Facing Reality

The shock of what was revealed during hypnotic regression left me dazed and distraught. Was I losing my mind? How was something like this possible? Could I have fabricated such a detailed account while under hypnosis? These and many other troubling questions crowded my thoughts for days after the session.

A chance conversation with the relatives I had been visiting at Montauk that fateful day, left me even more unnerved. As I described the "door in the hill" I had viewed near a cliff, my cousin stated she had come upon an area very similar to what I depicted, while walking near the Lighthouse one afternoon. I knew then, with complete certainty, that I needed to find the "door in the hill" in order to provide myself with validation of this experience.

I returned to Montauk on Sunday, December 17, 1995 with my friend Bill, an investigator for MUFON, and his wife. Bill understood my intense need to find "the door in the hill" in order to come to grips with my memories of that fateful day 25 years ago. When we arrived at Montauk, we first went down Old Montauk Highway...the road Louise and I took at the end of our "tour". Bill asked me to let them know when I felt we were entering the "void". I felt it much stronger than I did the first time. I let him know when it ended and the ominous feeling began. At the end of the road, the wood chip pile visible on our last visit had been cleared away and the road opened again. It looked like an area of brush and trees had been cleared completely...very strange. I could not make myself get out of the car; my fear was that intense.

As we started back on the road in the direction from which we came, a police car drove past us. This seemed quite unusual, as this road is isolated with no thru traffic. Had our arrival caused concern? Before we reached the "void" on our return trip, I suggested that Bill use the electromagnetic field detector he had brought to see if we got any readings. He gave it to me and asked that I let them know when I "felt" we were entering the void. I told them I felt it starting...a few seconds later, the light on the device went from green to amber. I said it was getting very strong...again maybe 3 seconds passed and the light went from amber to red. Then the device went crazy, flashing like a pinball machine! As we started to exit the void, I continued to give my "readings", confirmed by the device a few seconds later.

We drove to the main highway and pulled off in the rest area. The three of us were almost too shocked to speak. Bill confided that he had been very skeptical of my ability to "feel" this void when we started this trip. He was now completely convinced. We proceeded to the lighthouse and parked the car.

As we walked down a rocky path to the beach, we noticed a crude handwritten sign advising that an erosion control project was ongoing in that area. Recently placed boulders and cement slabs were evident. At this point, my "feelings" were at the most intense level I had ever felt. There was something about the placement of these of these boulders and slabs that wasn't "right". I was drawn to a point above the beach...a cliff jutting out over the sand.

We left the beach and walked up a hill towards the parking area Louise and I walked to our last visit. The whole time we were on the beach, I had the feeling we were being watched and I mentioned this to Bill. Just before we reached the parking area, I observed a man crouching in the brush on the top of a hill and I pointed him out to Bill. The man stood up and stared at us. Bill took out his camera and took his picture. The man crouched down again and eventually was lost from view. We did not encounter him again.

Only a few hundred feet from the hill was the parking area on the cliff. Looking to the west-northwest was Camp Hero. This was the vicinity my cousin stated seeing a door, similar to the one I had described. I looked around and saw what appeared to be a partial view of a stone and mortar wall. This had to be the door! I felt something about it, but I was confused... it just didn't seem right somehow. I remembered the hill being much higher and more pronounced. I started to wander away from Bill and his wife... going back toward the lighthouse. I was walking on the opposite side of the hill where we had spotted the man...closer to the ocean and the cliff.

I stopped every few yards and looked out over the ocean and tried to compare the image with what I had recalled. My feelings of helplessness and terror were very intense at this point. I continued to walk further back towards the lighthouse. Suddenly, I was standing in front of it...THE DOOR...exactly as I had remembered it! I shouted for Bill and his wife. They came and seemed stunned by what they saw. I started to cry, and everything I had bottled up for so long came out. It was such a relief. I now knew, with complete certainty, that my experience had been real. I was not losing my mind or imagining things.

Next to the door was a small opening that leads to a short tunnel. The end of the tunnel had been cemented over. On the ground, in front of the door, was a concrete circle, divided into equal parts including an equal section in the center of the circle. It was approximately 8-10 feet in diameter. There was a red fire hydrant next to it. Anchored from a utility pole on the other side of the hill and almost completely outlining the circumference of the hill stretched a thick, black electrical wire. This wire ended abruptly, tied to a bush. Looking over the cliff, wires running from inside the cliff, hung down about 10 feet and then snaked back inside the cliff. There were remnants of a structure or building at the top of the hill, above the door. Photographs were taken of the entire area from different angles.

As we departed the area, I spotted from the road, a section that seemed devoid of any trees or brush. While Bill waited on the road, I climbed down into the thick brush, to investigate. Finally breaking clear, I found a large, circular area of what appeared to be dead, crushed grass, interspersed with taller clumps that looked as if they had been chopped or cut down. The trees that bordered this area also appeared dead. Hidden in a thicket of bushes, just to the west of the circle, was a group of large boulders, similar to those evident on the beach. The arrangement of the boulders immediately brought an image of "table and chairs" to my mind. Several trees next to the boulders had been uprooted completely. It was apparent that these boulders were not a natural formation, and had been placed in this location. But how – and more importantly, why?

Further Validation

Recently, I was able to view video tapes filmed by Preston Nichols, of the underground facilities at Montauk prior to them being sealed. They contained footage that he did NOT include on the videos produced for sale to the public. One of the cassettes contained footage of the bunker I brought into, what I have come to call my "door in the hill". I sat, as if in a trance, and viewed the familiar images on the screen...the large entrance area behind "the door"...the "bright hallway" (white) beyond the entrance area... small rooms located off the hallway.

Although I remembered the hallway being longer, and a small alcove where an elevator had been located, it was possible that a wall had been constructed at what appeared to be the dead end. I had already confirmed the existence of an elevator in this location with a retired military intelligence officer familiar with Camp Hero's underground facilities during the period 1954-58.

Here was further validation of my account! I should have been elated. Instead, I found myself sitting there quietly, a knot in my stomach, saying to myself, "My God...it is REAL!" It doesn't seem to matter how much validation I receive...I don't want to believe what I know to be true.

Also while viewing these videotapes; I had a conscious recall of being contained in an isolation tank. This flashback included seeing a "face" of a person (human) familiar to me, and a telepathic conversation meant to calm and soothe me. During the conversation, he referred to me as "little one".

I met with Dr. Kouguell a few days later to explore this memory through hypnotic regression. From the moment he asked during the session if I was sure I wanted to look at this memory, a battle was waged in my mind. He asked me to indicate "yes" by slightly moving my right index finger. And try as hard as I could, I could not move it. Then he asked me to indicate "no" by slightly moving my right middle finger. It took all my power to hold it in place. I finally moved my right index finger ever so slightly. I had never had this experience while under hypnosis before.

I recalled being in a dark place...being afraid...floating in something that felt slightly heavier than water...feeling warm...and smelling peppermint or spearmint. He took me to a point before being in that place. I was lying naked on a table and had a lot of wires attached to me, all over my body and my head. I saw "that doctor" in a white lab coat standing next to me. Then he took me to a point before I was there. I was home in my room (different home than now). I woke up and 2 men dressed in black clothes were in my room. I couldn't see anything of what they looked like.

I asked where Joe and David were (my roommates). I was told they were sleeping. I was then given an injection and felt very sleepy. I was wrapped in a blanket and carried out the back door to a dark van (blue?). I was placed on the floor in the rear of the van and someone sat near me. The next thing I remember is feeling as if I were on a roller coaster. I don't know where I was taken or how long it took to get there. Suddenly, I was standing naked in front of a metal door, struggling with a soldier holding a rifle, while "that doctor" told me I "had to do this". I was sobbing, pleading with him not to "make me go back in there".

I couldn't continue with the session and Dr. Kouguell brought me back. I told him, as much as I wanted to remember what happened, I knew I wasn't ready yet to face it. Eventually, I knew I would have to.

An agonizing dilemma ensued. Conscious of my need to find the truth of my involvement, could I actually be unable to face it? What if my reluctance to explore this memory was being controlled by outside influences? The battle continued to rage in my mind until I finally made the decision to continue...I had come too far to turn back now. I would face the truth and rely on my strength of conviction to overcome any obstacles.

Before we began the next regression, I related my observations on possible "blocks" of this memory to Dr. K. I suggested a deep-level trance might be needed to retrieve them. While under hypnosis, I started to "relive" this experience.

I am, once again, in a black enclosed area...struggling, afraid of drowning. Why do I have to be in this place? It scares me so much...I want to get out! I calm myself enough to float. The liquid feels heavier than water. It's warm and I smell something "minty". I can feel wires attached to me as I move my arms and legs slightly...on my chest and head, too. I stretch out my arms, trying to feel the walls that enclose me. On my

Commander X's Guide to Incredible Conspiracies

right, my fingers trace the smooth surface, travelling upwards in an arc above me. Floating...gentle motion...blackness all around...are my eyes open, or are they closed? Is this 'blackness' I see only in my mind?

I can see movement...forms and shadows. Blackness lightens to dark gray. My friend is here and says, "Don't be afraid, little one. I will help you ...guide you...take my hand". Dark gray now turning to blue, like the sky ...white clouds. It feels like I'm flying. I can see a beautiful, lush hilltop, overlooking tranquil blue water. A large white building (a house?) with tall pillars and steps sits on top of the hill. A dirt road is nearby, and I can see a man, dressed in a short tunic, struggles to move a wooden cart. Scenes flashing...bright swirl of colors, orange, red, deep purple and shades of brown and tan.

I see a rocky, mountainous area...dry like the desert, dusty. There are deep canyons...high cliffs. Scenes flashing...diving through the white foam of a dark blue wave. I am underwater, among the sea creatures. But it's light and I can see beautiful colors. There is a dark entrance to what looks like a cave among the hills and rocks. Scenes flashing...a desolate place...not a nice feeling...barren...lonely...cold...a place out of time. Time is not what we think. Each moment is happening now...on an endless 'loop'. We can enter the loops at many points...but should take care not to disrupt the loops. Past, present and future are happening simultaneously.

After the session, I discussed what I had retrieved with Dr. Kouguell. Although, I was filled with wonder and awe at what I had experienced, unable to be sure if it had happened in the past or present, I still felt I had not been given a "choice" about participating. Dr. K. mentioned the fact that I had willingly "taken" my friend's hand...wasn't that making a choice?

I explained my feelings using the following analogy...If someone was dangling me by my feet off the 13th story of a building, threatening to drop me, and along comes a man on a flying carpet, offering to save me...is that REALLY a choice? Or am I being coerced to follow a certain direction? After some discussion, I came to the understanding that I now have a choice. I'm able to jump from that "13 story building". I know I will not fall!

Michelle Guerin is from Point Lookout, NY, and is interested in
UFO's, Abductions, Time Travel and Powers of the Mind
http://members.aol.com/nymush/sands.html

Commander X's Guide to Incredible Conspiracies

The SUB-ROSA "Reptoid"/ Inner Earth and DRAC Conspiracy
By "TAL" (ZON)

[Latin "SUB-ROSA", under the Rose (from the practice of hanging a rose over a meeting, as a symbol of confidentiality)

* In secret; privately or covertly: "They held the meetings sub rosa, to avoid general criticism."

OK...I have had direct face-to-face contact with the REPTOIDS. What have I learned? That THEY are NOT going to be openly coming back to the surface of the Planet, anytime soon.

They like it down there, in the Inner Earth. They do wish the UV protective "Cloud Canopy", around the Earth, would return. (To "create one" may be another "Conspiracy" that is going on.)

I learned that they have had "on going" Trade Relations, with various groups of humans, for AGES. Also learned, that if you thought you had problems from the REPTOIDS (SERPENT RACE), in the Past, just wait...the Reptilian "Off Planet" Military forces (The DRAC/DRAGON Race) are RETURNING.

They are vast in numbers and most will be here by 2012. They don't take shit from anybody. They function well, using their "DRACONIAN Solutions".
Contrary to popular belief they don't eat humans, as a habit. But, the DRAC Warriors do eat "Any Species" that they are at War with. This is a Religious Ritual (Rite), not for a food source. So...don't piss them off.

The DRAC are returning to Breed (on their HOME WORLD...EARTH). They will pick up TRIBUTE, WATER and other Resources. * This is kind of a R&R stop (Rest & Relaxation). Then, they will LEAVE Again (Just after 2012).

The INNER EARTH REPTOIDS "respect" the Drac. But, some of the Hybrid-Greys have been working with Governments of the World and have been trying to get certain human military forces to Attack the Incoming DRAC. Some Greys don't like being subservient to the REPS.

No creatures, in the Universe, have EVER won a War with the DRAC. So...Keep your head down and relax. Humans should be HERE for Ages to come.

We WILL have to develop our relationship with the Inner Earth REPTOIDS, if the entire ecosystem, of this Planet, is to survive. We don't need the DRAC leaders to come up with a DRACONIAN Solution for the "Human Problem". WE NEED to get off the oil-based economy ASAP! This means that the human CORPORATE GREED System needs to be replaced...and SOON!

Even the small group of surviving Ancient ELDER Humans, who left the surface of the Planet (ages ago) for protection deep within the Earth, have been making contact since the 1950's and admonishing humans, on the surface of the Planet, to "GET IT TOGETHER". (No more Nukes!)

During the "Age of ZON" (pre-flood), there were groups of Reptilians and Humans that worked together. We may "openly" have to do this again, to survive. So...let's bring the SECRETS into the Light.

Open PUBLIC Contact with various Inner Earth Civilizations (and Outer Space cultures) is our real Heritage and Future. Let's bring back the BALANCE needed to progress.

Commander X's Guide to Incredible Conspiracies

OUTER/SURFACE/INNER Earth Beings UNITE, in Peace and Harmony. Set aside your Fears. What you see as an Outer CONFLICT is really a manifestation of an INNER Conflict.

Many people are out of contact with their Inner "Reptilian Nature". They are out of Balance with the various aspects of their OWN Beingness. The Reptoids and Humans have a common ancestor. DNA connects us. We are similar in many ways.

This mechanism of "form generation" is about all aspects of our higher selves, our bodies, our mind, our reptilian brain, emotional bodies, energetic bodies, the causal body, etc. In most likelihood, you have manifested more times as a "Reptilian Humanoid" than a Human, on this Planet. Learn anything yet?

Phil Servedio said it this way, "This is a war of the ugliest of kinds, and taking to extremes, extrapolated to a societal level, a cause of the wars between others, between tribes and nation-states. Our threatened existence, this fundamental conflict between two opposing FORCES INSIDE OF US is then played out on a larger battlefield, projecting the threat of our dissolution on the enemy (which of course can be most real and true, if someone or some state wants to annihilate you), on all levels of human existence. A barometer for psychological and spiritual maturity, in my opinion, is the capacity to withdraw those kind of projections from the 'other', be it a personal enemy or threat, 'the evil empire', the 'great Satan', whatever."

David Wheeler once said, "A better term for self-realization is self-resolution". The inner conflict, the subtle but antagonizing dilemma over opposing forces, that is really WITHIN us and our multiple nature is what drives the conflict. The mammalian-emotional brain and the more primal reptilian brain. Also, there are the conflicts of the Left Brain and a Right Brain.

WE need to resolve these conflicts within us. We have a opportunity for PEACE (Balance), Healing and Enlightenment. We should find more constructive ways to deal with our inner conflicts and move beyond "the either-or", into "the as-well-as".

To become more and more flexible so that we can adapt to the ever-changing flow of LIFE and to take care of the negative thoughts in our mind. We are the real CONSPIRACY and it is against ourselves. So, no more CONSPIRACIES (of the harmful kind).

SIDE NOTE: Sun: Hebrew "ZON" or "ZAWON", to "encircle", becomes in Chaldee DON or dawon. In Celtic, DON or DAN. In early Chaldean, Shemesh, meaning "the servant". The name Tor, "the revolver", in reference to the sun is a synonym of the Greek "ZEN" or "ZAN" applied to Jupiter which signifies "the encircler" or "encompasser". Origin of the word SUN. In Anglo-Saxon, sunna, and in Egypt the term snnus refers to the sun's orbit.

In Egyptian, the terms "ZON" & "ON" was used, before the term "RA" was. HoriZON ZONe HOR-I-ZON-TAL = horizontal (HORus).

SIDE NOTE: "AUM" (normally written in Greek transliteration "IAO"). "IAO" stands for "ISIS (Auset) - Apophis – OSIRIS (Ausar)". Au = Symbol of GOLD * IAO is a generalized formula of consecration. One takes a material basis (I = Isis = nature or matter) and applies magickal energy to it (A = Apophis = ENERGY), raising its rate of vibration and producing an influential radiance (O = Osiris = SOL = ON = "ZON").

Note: Osiris was and is one of the first "Green Men", in that he was also the god of vegetation. *Os-IRIS taught "Farming".

NOTE: The Serpent "Typhon-Set-Satan(Sat-an)-SamaEL-Lucifer" killed his brother Osiris. Typhon-Set is said to be 'the opponent force" or the 'accuser". The name Seth with the syllable AN from the Chaldean ANA or Heaven, makes the term Satan (Set-AN). Satan from the verb "Sitan", to oppose.

The alchemical formula of "I.A.O", Isis, Apophis, Osiris [Birth, Death, resurrection...or the CYCLE of life, death, and rebirth.] is to the Adept, a powerful process of transformation that unlocks the keys of magical power and of immortality.
On Jules Verne's grave are carved the words, "ONward Towards Immortality".

ZONULE = A small zone. A power area. The center of a Zonule. Around the CENTER, there is the magick CIRCLE where few will dare to enter.

The Circle is quartered...Earth, Air, Fire and Water. YHVH = the Circle-Cross.
The CIRCLE-CROSS: "INRI": an important acronym in both orthodox religion and in magic. The initials are attributed to the initials to the first letters of certain Hebrew words used to describe the four elements (I - Yam - Water; N - Nour - Fire; R - Ruach - Air; I - Yebeshah - Earth). INRI is known as the "Keyword" and is used to describe the cycle of the seasons; the equinoxes and solstices, as well as the cycles of birth, death, and rebirth (I - Yod - Virgo; N - Nun - Scorpio; R - Resh - the Sun; I - Yod - Virgo).

For when the four mundane elements are assembled, the FIFTH ELEMENT (the Will) becomes more powerful. * For the cosmic mind is THE MATRIX, of the fifth dimension.

The Fifth Column of ZON. Note: Take the letter "Z" and put it within an "O", so they touch. Now, put in the letter "N". What you see is a Circle quartered. Which looks like PYRAMID, within a CIRCLE. The very center point is the "Gateway"; the "TRANS-FINITE POINT"; "Key zONE" of the Fifth Element; Spirit/Ether = OM or AUM (A Mantra Characterizing The Supreme Power) * "AUM" (normally written in Greek transliteration "IAO").

* The Christ dies on the CROSS of Matter, to open the PORTAL to GOD (The Divine Source). "ZON" = Spiritual Warrior.

NOTE: I am an Independent "INFORMATION EXCHANGER". If you have located Material related to the above, please SHARE it with others.

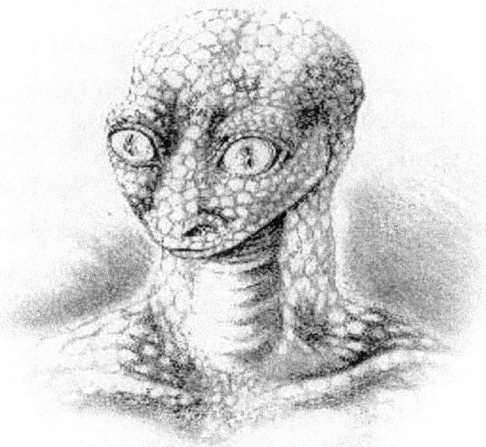

The Secret Covenant of the Reptilians
By U. Author

This covenant is sealed by blood, our blood. An illusion it will be, so large, so vast it will escape their perception. Those who will see it will be thought of as insane. We will create separate fronts to prevent them from seeing the connection between us.

We will behave as if we are not connected to keep the illusion alive. Our goal will be accomplished one drop at a time so as to never bring suspicion upon us. This will also prevent them from seeing the changes as they occur. We will always stand above the relative field of their experience for we know the secrets of the absolute. We will work together always and will remain bound by blood and secrecy. Death will come to he who speaks. We will keep their lifespan short and their minds weak. We will use our knowledge of science and technology in subtle ways so they will never see what is happening. We will use soft metals, aging accelerators and sedatives in food and water, also in the air. The soft metals will cause them to lose their minds. We will promise to find a cure from our many fronts, yet we will feed them more poison.

The poisons will be absorbed through their skin and mouth's, they will destroy their minds and reproductive systems. From all this, their children will be born dead, and we will conceal this information. The poisons will be hidden in everything that surrounds them, in what they drink, eat, breathe and wear. We must be ingenious in dispensing the poisons for they can see far. We will teach them that the poisons are good, with fun images and musical tones. Those they admire will help to push our poisons.

They will see our products being used in film and will grow accustomed to them and will never know their true effect. When they give birth we will inject poisons into the blood of their children and convince them it's for their help. We will start early on, when their minds are young, we will target their children with what children love most, sweet things. We will render them docile and weak before us by our power. They will grow depressed, slow and obese, and when they come to us for help, we will give them more poison. We will focus their attention toward money and material goods so they many never connect with their inner self. We will distract them with fornication, external pleasures and games so they may never be one with the oneness of it all.

Their minds will belong to us and they will do as we say. If they refuse we shall find ways to implement mind-altering technology into their lives. We will use fear as our weapon. We will establish their governments and establish opposites within. We will own both sides. We will always hide our objective but carry out our plan. They will perform the labor for us and we shall prosper from their toil. Our families will never mix with theirs. Our blood must be pure always, for it is the way. We will make them kill each other when it suits us. We will keep them separated from the oneness by dogma and religion. We will control all aspects of their lives and tell them what to think and how. We will guide them kindly and gently letting them think they are guiding themselves.

We will foment animosity between them through our factions. When a light shall shine among them, we shall extinguish it by ridicule, or death, whichever suits us. We will make them rip each other's hearts apart and kill their own children. We will accomplish this by using hate as our ally, anger as our friend. The hate will blind them totally, and never shall they see that from their conflicts we emerge as their rulers. They will be busy killing each other.

Commander X's Guide to Incredible Conspiracies

They will bathe in their own blood and kill their neighbors for as long as we see fit. We will benefit greatly from this, for they will not see us, for they cannot see us. We will continue to prosper from their wars and their deaths. We shall repeat this over and over until our ultimate goal is accomplished. We will continue to make them live in fear and anger though images and sounds.

We will make them hate themselves and their neighbors. We will always hide the divine truth from them, that we are all one. This they must never know! They must never know that color is an illusion. They must always think they are not equal. Drop by drop we will advance our goal. We will take over their land, resources and wealth to exercise total control over them.

We will deceive them into accepting laws that will steal the little freedom they will have. We will establish a money system that will imprison them forever, keeping them and their children in debt. When they shall ban together, we shall accuse them of crimes and present a different story to the world for we shall own all the media. We will use our media to control the flow of information and their sentiment in our favor.

When they shall rise up against us we will crush them like insects, for they are less than that. They will be helpless to do anything for they will have no weapons. We will recruit some of their own to carry out our plans, we will promise them eternal life, but eternal life they will never have for they are not of us.

The recruits will be called "initiates" and will be indoctrinated to believe false rites of passage to higher realms. Members of these groups will think they are one with us never knowing the truth. They must never learn this truth for they will turn against us. For their work they will be rewarded with earthly things and great titles, but never will they become immortal and join us, never will they receive the light and travel the stars. They will never reach the higher realms, for the killing of their own kind will prevent passage to the realm of enlightenment. This they will never know. The truth will be hidden in their face, so close they will not be able to focus on it until its too late.

Oh yes, so grand the illusion of freedom will be, that they will never know they are our slaves. When all is in place, the reality we will have created for them will own them. This reality will be their poison. They will live in self-delusion. When our goal is accomplished a new era of domination will begin. Their minds will be bound by their beliefs, the beliefs we have established from time immemorial. But if they ever find out they are our equal, we shall perish then. THIS THEY MUST NEVER KNOW.

If they ever find out that together they can vanquish us, they will take action. They must never, ever find out what we have done, for if they do, we shall have no place to run, for it will be easy to see who we are once the veil has fallen. Our actions will have revealed who we are and they will hunt us down and no person shall give us shelter.

This is the secret covenant by which we shall live the rest of our present and future lives, for this reality will transcend many generations and life spans.

This covenant is sealed by blood, our blood. We, the ones who from heaven to earth came. This covenant must NEVER, EVER be known to exist. It must NEVER, EVER be written or spoken of for if it is, the consciousness it will spawn will release the fury of the PRIME CREATOR upon us and we shall be cast to the depths from whence we came and remain there until the end time of infinity itself.

Commander X's Guide to Incredible Conspiracies

The Shape-Shifting Myth and Mystery
Wm. Michael Mott

One of the oldest types of entities in folkloric and mythological accounts is also one of the latest, and of late, more common in paranormal or fortean accounts. Various entities may, upon initial consideration of witness accounts, seem widely-disparate in nature; yet whether of "gray" alien, the original Puerto Rican "chupacabras," "grinning men" (of various sizes, heights and descriptions), MIBs, or "reptoid" type, all seem to share a variety of characteristics which can be more or less identifiable as "reptilian" or "amphibian" in nature. These characteristics range from "leathery" or lizard-like skin texture, bulging eyes, slit or oblique pupils, webbed hands or fingers, and to some extent, sparseness or absence of facial and body hair.

The reptilians or "reptoids," stretching back through the centuries, have had a folkloric reputation of being deceivers, shapeshifters, vampires, and anthropophagous. Sightings and encounters have provided the basis for legends of horned, leathery demons and imps; goblins; ghuls; "henkies" and other dwarfish, somewhat-humanoid forms, nagas, trolls, and so on. The interest in human blood and genetic materials, exhibited by fairy lovers and abductors, elves, trolls, undines, incubi, succubi, frog princes, jinn, "deros," and the elemental or sylph-like "gray aliens" is all too obvious.

Of particular interest is the ability, currently attributed to the "reptoids" or lizard-men of ufological and conspiracy accounts, to "shape-shift" or take on an illusion of humanity. Some accounts have the reality the other way, in which the human being, due to stimulation of an non-human bloodlust or other desire, is transformed or "shifted" into a reptilian humanoid. While the latter type of "sighting," when genuine, may indicate a form of demonic (spiritually "reptilian") possession or oppression which is so powerful as to be visible for a temporary time in the visible spectrum, it is not necessarily the same as the encounters reported, through the centuries, of "real" shape-shifters, reptilians, devils, fairies, and "aliens" which can take on a deceptive or even a familiar form, for purposes of predation.

The ability of the fairies or "good neighbors" (a euphemism) to use "glamour," of nagas and rakshasas to utilize sorcerous illusion, and "vampires" and their "hypnotic" and shape-changing abilities, are reflected, in modern variants, in the reports of shape-shifting reptoid imposters, alien abductors who appear as familiar friends or family members, or the "rays" generated by dero "mech" which create a holographic persona. What is the "true nature" of these beings, and what is their common link, if any?

In the book "Etidorpha," a man is taken on a tour of the underworld and cavern realms by a "guide" who is more or less humanoid in form, but is described as having skin or flesh of an amphibian-like texture and no body hair whatsoever. This being is also compared to a lizard, and is described as being "slimy," "cold and clammy," and so on. The "guide" has one distinguishing characteristic which stands out in particular, however: "he" has no face at all, just a smooth ovoid patch where a face should be. As it turns out, he is not alone.

"Faceless" entities have long been present in apparition, ghost, and monster stories. Could these forms have any relation to the "shape-shifting" types of beings described? Are they not just reptilians, but representatives of a type of life which is both parasitic and chameleon-like? The question which comes forward is this: Could a "faceless" form of "genome-thief" still not be essentially reptilian, or a type of

Commander X's Guide to Incredible Conspiracies

mammalian/reptilian creature descended from reptiles (as we humans, and all mammals, supposedly are)? Chameleons alter their skins cells to reflect colors, patterns, and even moods like aggression or passivity; could there be a form of life which has evolved this to an ultimate form of mimicry or deception, actually using stolen or absorbed genetic material? Would this possibility provide an answer to MANY mysteries?

There must be a clue, an explanation as to the "malleability" of these beings, their transformational abilities or else powers of genetic manipulation. Perhaps some of them are like "blank genetic templates," upon which an entire genome can be temporarily or permanently imprinted; or even different types of genomes, stolen from other life forms, are imprinted or combined. Here would be an answer to the chimaerical and "hybrid" forms of many of the more outrageous "goblins," "cryptids" and ufonauts!

In an October 20, 1991 lecture, Ufologist Michael Lindemann delivered a lecture which contained this first-person witness account of an encounter in a top-secret underground military site:

"My friend who worked in the underground bases, who was doing sheet-rock was down on, he thinks, approximately the 30th level underground... these bases are perhaps 30-35 stories deep. As I say they are not just mine shafts, these are huge, giant facilities... many city blocks in circumference, able to house tens of thousands of people. One of them, the YANO Facility [we're told... by the county fire dept. director, the county fire dept. chief who had to go in there to look at a minor fire infraction] there's a 400-car parking lot on the 1st level of the YANO Facility, but cars never come in and out, those are the cars that they use INSIDE.

"O.K., so... a very interesting situation down there. Our guy was doing sheet-rock on the 30th floor, maybe the 30th floor, underground. He and his crew are working on a wall and right over here is an elevator door. The elevator door opens and, a kind of reflex action you look, and he saw three 'guys'. Two of them, human engineers that he's seen before. And between them a 'guy' that stood about 8 to 8 1/2 feet tall. Grey skin, extra-long arms, wearing a lab coat, holding a clip-board, AND HE DIDN"T HAVE A FACE! My friend said it was just teeth right there. Just teeth where a face should be..."

The Maya called such underworld shapeshifters "vhujunka." Other than the face, the physical description sounds much like that of one of the so-called reptoids reported at the alleged Dulce complex in New Mexico. Right down to the height, white lab-coat, and clipboard.

Are "reptilian" faces as much an illusion as anything else might be? Does this "faceless" account indicate that we're dealing with something that can appear in any form, or with any face, that it wishes? Underworld beings are traditionally the masters of "glamourie," or glamour, illusion, shape-shifting, deception, and so on, and of course, "Satan can appear even as an angel of light." But their interest in US is so self-serving and manipulative, yet tinged with desperation, that other questions logically follow.

Is it possible that we might be dealing with something which is PURELY A GENETIC THIEF OR PARASITE? A thief of genomes, in whole or in part as the necessity arises, a "blank slate" predator which can assume a variety of appearances? As noted previously and repetitively, this has traditionally been the province of "underworld" or subterranean beings in folk traditions worldwide, from western fairies and demons, middle eastern jinn and dubuks, to Indian nagas and Japanese "foxes" or fox-people.

These "others" may be genetically diverse beyond our imagining, due to this ability, yet incapable of reproducing of their own accord, or maintaining a stable and comfortable face, form, or life-span without it...and how does this all tie in with both livestock and human mutilations, which are essentially identical in nature and tend to concentrate on the blood, mucous membranes, reproductive organs and surrounding tissues, eyes, "meaty" organs like the liver (which is highly regenerative), and so on? Could these materials be of particular importance to an advanced genome-imprinting or cloning technology, which utilizes genetic material that has been purloined from somewhere or someone else?

Perhaps they have perfected a form of tissue regeneration and repair which requires some of the same materials which have always been offered up in sacrifices to the dark, bloody "gods" of antiquity, and THIS is the secret to "their" longevity (remember, vampires "live" forever as long as they stay out of the sun, and sun-dodging fairies are generally considered "undying" as well). Gruesome photos of a human mutilation victim from Brazil, along with autopsy data, support yet again that the vital organs, along with the most successfully regenerative tissues--the blood, mucous membranes, glands, "sweet bread" organs (the often self-regenerative liver, as well as stomach, intestines, etc.), sexual organs, and so on--are always the focus of their selfish and brutal desires.

It seems at times that Keel, Steiger, and other researchers dance around this possibility and even hint at it, but never really come out and say it. Until now, it may simply have been too unspeakable to contemplate or dare to put into print.

Even if unseen manipulators and predators have a reptilian origin that's lost in a vast antiquity, could it be that they have a partially hominid, somewhat mammalian heritage as well? Could they be as closely related to humanity as the monotremes (egg-laying mammals) are to the vivverids, for instance? Are they an ancient form of predator, which is in fact a parasite, who has evolved along with all hominids, and culminating with a dependence upon modern humanity? Vaguely, distantly, related in the vertebrate sense, perhaps more reptilian than we mammals, yet so old a species or variety of specie that they have evolved beyond our labels, and now represent a third form which is divergent, to some degree, from both the reptilian and mammalian kingdoms; this indeed seems more plausible as time goes by.

We may need to re-evaluate the nature of our ancient enemies.

For more information, visit Wm. Michael Mott's website at:
http://home.earthlink.net/~mottimorph/SubterraneanIntro2.html

Commander X's Guide to Incredible Conspiracies

From the Garden
By Cassie

The subject of "good" vs. "bad" reptilians is such a broad issue but I feel it is necessary to make some sense of this confusion so we each know where we stand on these issues. More and more people are beginning to "wake up" and become aware that we have been infiltrated by beings that are not quite "human". These "para-humans" which are part human and part...something else...walk amongst us in human forms yet are perceived as spiritually altered hybrid humans by many people. There are many explanations I could go into here but I will make it as simple as possible.

The reptoid/dragon like species referred to here are very old, older than the human race...and they have probably walked among us since the beginnings of history. The Sumerian myths of origin...as well as creation myths of most of our cultures around the world exemplify this belief.

Somewhere down the line, they have interbred with humans and continue to do so to produce humans with reptilian DNA in varying degrees. What I am saying is that we are all part reptilian. Some people have more of the reptilian characteristics and instincts than others. These human/reptilian beings are hybrids...which make up most of the humans on our planet.

I have noticed several processes by which the reptilian essence incorporates into humans, other than breeding. None of this has to do with soul quality...which is what most of the disagreement on "good" vs. "evil" reptilians is all about and which I will get into later.

The first group is self-proclaimed reptilians that feel they are reincarnated or born into human bodies but are reptilians in spirit. These individuals, out of the ones I have come into contact with are very aware of who they are. They are highly intelligent generally; yet exhibit many of the instinctual reptilian characteristics. This group possesses an insight into their nature and most are on a personal mission to find their niche in the human world. Many suffer from existential angst or depression...deep feelings of inferiority...but just as humans use this depression to grow emotionally, so do these reptilians. I have actually found this particular group to be the most advanced and fun to interact with. I have learned a lot about them and their nature from this group. I will refer to this group as "Group A".

The second group is a much broader group, as they don't really have an assigned "human" form. These manifest themselves sometimes as actual humanoid reptilians or reptoids but have a prime interdimensional core to them. These guys look for vulnerable human hybrid bodies or "Hosts" to inhabit and try to live a somewhat normal existence through the host.

This process in itself is an invasive activity, but at the same time is looked upon as SURVIVAL that they feel is the norm. They do not inhabit the human bodies all the time but linger about for waiting for opportune moments when the host has breaks in their spirit bodies that allow for the reptilians to enter.

Human's who have these reptilian "handlers" hanging about may experience them in nocturnal attacks, incubus experiences or even channeled "guides" sometimes friendly and sometimes not so friendly. I'll call this group "Group B" reptilians. It is my personal belief that these particular reptilians when not inhabiting their "hosts" are living

Commander X's Guide to Incredible Conspiracies

underground where survival is easier for them. Unless of course they find residing within human bodies serves their personal agendas of the moment.

The Tilt of the Scales, or Good Vs. Evil

When describing reptilians by herpetologist definitions, one can see the instinct driven natures of this species, their ambitions to excel regardless of the consequences, their lack of normal human emotion or values, their mating habits or gender confusion using a human body. Their adrenaline-based reactions seem to take place of emotions, as we know them. These reptilians can be the highest of achievers...or the darkest of deceivers.

The reptilian's values differ from men at the deepest core level, in that the superficial achievements, their attainment of materials things, their conquests and their dominance are what they strive for. They are great egotists as well, looking down on humans as inferior. The reptilians do not play by the same rules that we do...they have different boundaries or social mores and therefore fewer self imposed restrictions on their behaviors. They have little use for such things as love relationships, admiration based on integrity, morals or philanthropic endeavors. They look at those human values as weaknesses. These differences in themselves do not make reptilians "evil" or humans "good". There is another element involved here.

One might question why the herpetic imaging...why the dragons, snakes and alligator images to depict these creatures? This motif was carefully chosen probably around the same time the Garden of Eden was created. Out of all the beasts and creatures of the time, the one who was most suited to depict lower base natures of darker forces was the reptile.

Satan chose the reptile to act out his wishes and manipulations upon mankind in order to work against God. Satan's point was to show God that mankind was nothing more than a mere instinctual animal, not made in His image as God intended. The snake was "hosted" by one of the "fallen angels" that led to the Fall of Man and Adam and Eve's expulsion from Eden.

The Battle For Your Soul

In today's world, Satan continues to spit in the face of God with lies, deceptions, and manipulations of humans using the less evolved reptilians. It is Satan's legions that take on the images of the dinosaur which speaks to men and manipulates him into being "less than" who he truly is, forcing men to lose sight of their inner light. This becomes a "Battle for the Soul" which is acted out by well meaning righteous individuals fighting both sides of this issue. As we all have elements of both man and animal/reptilian within our genes, we still have free will to create our lifestyles so they are not so open to demonic attack.

Those who are in Group A, the reincarnated reptilians in human bodies will need to fight harder against the demonic manipulation. Demons look for weaknesses within our spirit...and they will surely use Group A's feelings of dislocation and isolation against them. Group A has a great advantage that most humans do not. They have the awareness of who they truly are and an innate understanding of both sides of the issues at hand. They also have the drive and the intellect to overcome the trickery at hand. This group will be essential in our planet's survival. The only hindrance might be the ego factor...the same trick pulled on Eve in the Garden.

As for Group B, there will be heroic scenarios acted out battling these demonic ones, and there will be great evil acted out as well. The outcome depends upon the soul quality of the individual who is used as a host...and the faith he/she holds. Those with certain personality disorders will have a worse time and be more predisposed to being hosted. The most common personality disorders associated with the "bad reptilians" are Narcissistic Personality Disorder, Anti-social Personality Disorder, and Borderline Personality Disorder, or a combination of any of these. The following descriptions of these personality disorders came from the DSM-IV, 4th edition.

Dependent Personality Disorder usually manifests itself in today's culture with substance abuse such as methamphetamine addiction or alcoholism. Narcissism usually displays a pattern of grandiosity and entitlement, a preoccupation of fantasies of unlimited success, power or brilliance, exhibits interpersonal exploitative behavior to others to meet own ends, and believes he is "special" and only understood by other special high-status people, and shows a lack of empathy for others. He will also display arrogance, with beliefs that others are envious of him while he is in truth envious of them. Anti-social Personalities usually display deceitfulness, repeated lying, conning others, extreme aggressiveness, reckless disregard for the safety of others, irresponsibility and lack of remorse demonstrated by indifference to or rationalization of hurting, mistreating or stealing from another.

Borderline Personality Disorder is exhibited by a pattern of unstable and intense interpersonal relationships characterized by extremes of devaluation and idealization. Frantic efforts to avoid real or imagined abandonment, identity disturbance, unstable self image, impulsivity in at least two areas that are self damaging (spending, sex, substance abuse, reckless driving, binge eating). Recurrent suicidal behavior, or self-mutilating behaviors. Chronic feelings of emptiness, inappropriate, intense anger with displays of temper and or physical fights, paranoid ideation or severe dissociative symptoms. Also, affective instability due to a marked reactivity of mood.

There are medications that can lessen the severity of these symptoms as well as counseling for "reality" checks. A personality disorder is not easily cured by either, as it is a lifelong pattern of reacting and becomes a component of the personality. These are the ones that seem most predisposed to hosting though.

Unfortunately, no one is immune to the hosting process. We all have times of troubles and ill health. I would bet every one of you who read this have a family member who is hosting a demon dressed in reptilian clothing. That is why we cannot abandon our hosty fellow humans. To abandon them is like allowing weeds to take over the garden. We must fight for them with our love. All beings can fight the negative forces that be. The first step is in awareness of the process to reduce mankind to animals. The second step is to know that no matter how lost you might feel you are, there is always hope. These beings (demons) have made fools of us all, but not for long. We have the power within us to raise above the manipulations...the dragon games. We have been made in God's image to walk in His path with Him. We have only to look upward, rise off our bellies and fly to the Father.

Email: psyche@cableone.net

EARTH AND CLIMATE CHANGES

Are the Polar Ice Caps Melting?
You Can Help Heal the Earth's Ancient Energy Grid
By Timothy Green Beckley

Taken from Magazine *Prophecies and Predictions for the New Millennium*

Facts About Elan: Elan O'Brien is the founder of the internationally recognized Inter-Dimensioning Healing. Her gifts were received from many ancient world cultures Inter-Dimensional awareness and wisdom were gifted in personal and direct contact with the whales and dolphins.

Many of the "light gods" and "codes" shared and facilitated in private sessions are a result of direct teachings from these great beings. Elan's work is powerful, poignant and profound, inciting union at the deepest levels of cells and soul.

She has done global work, assisting to share sacred ceremony in some of the planet's most ancient temples. She continues to travel worldwide, presenting profound healing and enlightenment in helping humankind in its transformation towards the next steps in creation, evolution and integration of the Divine Plan.

For information contact: Elan O'Brien, P0. Box 990, Indian Hills, Colorado 80454. Telephone: 303 - 697- 8811

Disembarking from the **Westedem** (the premier flag ship of the Holland America lines), Tim Beckley found himself along with New Age light worker Elan O'Brien walking across the polar ice shelf, said to be receding at the rate of nearly two miles per year. The end result could he a total melting of the poles, causing traumatic global consequences.

Q: I want to start out by just getting a little bit of background. What made you decide to come on this trip in a metaphysical view and what is your background as far as being involved in the whole spiritual awakening of planet Earth?

O'BRIEN: I guess to begin with I'll answer your second question first. And that is in terms of my own background and experience. About eleven years ago, after becoming fairly disillusioned with Senior Management and a Corporate Executive lifestyle, my "self" went through some dramatic personal changes and revelations after a trip to Egypt. And after that trip, I returned to leave my job. And then to follow some would say "inner guidance," others would say your "heart" and others would say "higher knowingness" or "intergalactic knowingness"-- and to travel the world for approximately eleven years. And most of that time, in the early stages, was spent simply going to specific points in the Earth as I was directed. And being in a position to experience what some would call "miracles," or what some would call "a higher unfolding." Basically, though, what it was working with as I came to understand later was the electromagnetic grids of planet Earth.

Q: And what are the electromagnetic grids of the planet? Where are they and how do you define them? Are they acknowledged by science? Or is this totally an intuitive thing?

O'BRIEN: Well, there is an acknowledgment of "ley lines" specific points throughout the earth. The electromagnetic grids are similar to ley lines but not exactly the same. They're more of a frequency or vibrational level that is around the planet. It's always been acknowledged as being "outside" for quite some time. And I also know it to be beneath the planet as well. So it's above and below. And it holds certain frequency bands, certain "energetics" of electromagnetics. So some people liken the electromagnetic grid to the nervous system of our bodies. It is not noticeable per se visibly, but it definitely is like a transmitter system or a carrier system.

Another way people can describe it is as looking almost like some of the AT&T commercials you see on your television. With these links or lines of light that spread right over the globe.

One of the ways it was first brought to light was in a book written by an author named John Nesbith called Megatrends, sometime ago. And what he found before they had any awareness of electromagnetic grid lines or anything of that nature he found by looking at newspapers that when a small, little obscure story happened in somewhere like Iowa, often almost the identical sort of story would be happening in another very distant place. Maybe in Maine or in Florida or Virginia.

The interest in this, what he started to find, was that there was like a common link of consciousness. So one of the best ways to describe the electromagnetic grid lines is that perhaps, in your own life, if you've ever had this great idea and for one reason or another didn't go ahead with it, and then in maybe less than six months found someone else had approximately the same timing, had developed or created the same thing you had thought of, that's a pretty good explanation of the grid lines. That it's almost like a highway or a link of consciousness or "beingness", a state that correlates into the body, that we can tap into. As we as humans or as a species and as a connection with the earth raise our vibration, then there is a direct correlation within this electromagnetic grid line. In other words, we can access more ideas, greater healing, greater senses of well-being, and a great affinity with the planet in connecting back to our own unique source within.

Q: Now. I take it that our understanding of these grid lines may have slipped away from us in recent centuries. This is a knowledge that was possessed by the ancients, perhaps the shamans, or the wise people that existed among the Druids or some of the ancient civilizations Egypt and so forth. Is this why Stonehenge and the pyramids and so forth were built on the locations where they were built…to draw this energy?

O'BRIEN: Well, there are different discussions about that. Some of those correlations are definitely believed to be true. The skill with navigation through the stars that so many of the Tahitians and Polynesians used to do with their canoes. So many of the Hawaiians even. The same with Stonehenge. But this links not only our planet Earth. What the real focus is here is it's also the harmonics that relate with our galactic presence.

Q: And what is this 'galactic presence'?

O'BRIEN: The knowingness that all aspects of us exist as an energy form in All That Is. And that we as human beings are here now the belief and the knowingness is that we are here on this planet with the capability of linking into parts of ourselves or energies which are aspects of self that relate in inter-dimensional and intergalactic consciousness realms. So, yes, there is an aspect of ourselves that when we tap into can correlate to some of the wisdom of the ancient faces on Mars. Some of the knowingness of what the rings of Saturn represent.

Q: Well, what do they represent?

O'BRIEN: Depending on our own belief system and where our focus is on this planet and what our consciousness and what our reality is they can represent a lot of things. But the primary thing that they represent is a connectedness, interrelatedness – a merging of inter-species evolution.

Q: Now, you have traveled around the world for the last eleven years, going to some of these key grid points. Where are the grid points? Where have you gone and what are some of the experiences that you've had there?

O'BRIEN: Some of the key grid points that I've come to learn about have been fairly vast and diverse. I had a lot of teachings through the whales that exist in the wild. And a lot of that information came through both Hawaii and Australia. So those were two of the major points. What I understood is that the whales themselves are higher evolutionary beings and they are working with the grid points from beneath the surfaces of the earth. Their communication, the way that sound moves through water is actually a model for The Source, which some people believe is the means by which the Universe creates itself.

My understanding, through the information and the wisdom of the whales, is that they were creating, from beneath the surfaces, a charge or a communication of consciousness and interconnectedness that we are still to come understand. They themselves have the knowingness of the greater "Oneness" it we are all looking to move back into and remember as opposed to the illusions of separation that we've played it for so long on this planet.

Their movements and their sounds part of working with those key grid points. And Hawaii and Australia were part of what we call "The Rainbow link" in several key grid points of the planet. Others were in Egypt and Ecuador. Another was in Bali or Indonesia, which was a center-point of the ring of Fire on the planet.

All of these points were what we would call "Key areas" or what were deemed by some as 'Key Areas Of Return For The Brotherhood And Sisterhood Of Light." In other words, the portal to allow a certain frequency to interconnect into our humanness in a way that was coming to a critical point up until this time. They also held the form, or even though it was a formless sort of structure, the form or the portal for some of the key areas of evolution. And, at this point in time, my key interest in going up to Alaska was that Alaska was one of the last of twelve major grid points that was to be opened that would allow a lot of the old structures that had been held fixed in our consciousness allowing us play out all these illusions of separation to open. Now that that has been opened, then we at this point in time can make some radical leaps in evolution.

Q: Maybe we can go to the map later on and actually pinpoint some of the locations of the grids. Now, you mentioned earlier, at the beginning of the interview, that you had an experience that kind of transformed your life that happened in Egypt that made you give up your life as a corporate executive and become attuned to the more spiritual. What exactly happened to you in Egypt?

O'BRIEN: In Egypt, it was what some would call an "activation of the blood crystals." Others would just call it an awakening. For me, it was a remembrance of who I was in a greater sense and why I had come to be here, and that even the corporate lifestyle had served me in a certain way. It was part of my journey. And my belief is that, for every individual, true power comes from knowing your total journey. The true power of your love knows that, no matter what you've chosen, it's still being part of the expression that you've come to remember. But after Egypt and the remembrance of initiations that I had...

Q: Are you talking about former lives?

O'BRIEN: Yeah.

Q: When were these former lives? What aspect was it? In other words, were you on an aspect now of something you were actually foretold, something that you were to do later on in another lifetime or today's life? Was this part of an overall program?

O'BRIEN: What I remembered was being part of a Malchizedek Order, which is what was called "The Scattered Brotherhood And Sisterhood Of Light:' it was an order of cosmic priests and priestesses. In actual fact, most people are members we have all served in Ancient Orders. No one of us is any better. We've all played all roles. We've all played all parts. But what I had remembered as my mission is that I had served many times in many lifetimes here on Earth but that my role here is what I call "galactic shamanism:' And that is acting to bring forward an interface for the other species that are linking harmonically to the Earth.

Q: So when you say these other species, are you talking about species that exist here, animal life on this planet? Or are we also to assume from that that there are beings from other planets that are coming here to help us in this evolution? And if so why would they necessarily be desirous of such an effect on us?

O'BRIEN: I'm actually speaking about all of it. The total interconnectedness and inter-relatedness, which we call "Oneness:' the reason that we're of such prime interest right now is, with what is happening on this planet. Earth is in what one would call a 'Kingpin Position." And never in the history of the universe that we know of has such a situation ever existed. And what it means is, as the vibration and the frequency of this planet and its inhabitants move forward, all other aspects and expressions are linked to it. They've been holding a balance and none of them can move forward until we do. Humankind stands at the crossroads to the Earth's future-many see it as the time of "sinking or swimming. So, therefore, that's why we have such acute interest from so many different other realms, so many different aspects. Be it the inter-dimensional, or be it even the animal kingdom, such as the whales and dolphins that we were talking about earlier.

Q: Have you had actual experiences with UFOs? Or the beings on board the ships? And if so, what sort of relationships have you had with them?

O'BRIEN: I've had a number of different experiences. Probably the one I that I would talk about was an experience I had during an acupuncture session where my consciousness was actually taken on board a ship. And I remembered the beings who were there, who were highly benevolent, and who instructed me as far as aspects of myself that were of them, and of my choices to be here now.

Q: Now that's a somewhat confusing statement. Can you elaborate on that a little bit more? Are you saying that you were actually someone from somewhere else who's here to do some work, or part of an aspect of someone else?

O'BRIEN: I'm saying that we all exist in All – and that parts of us energetically exist in All Connections. One of the reasons for my belief in the inter-species connection and the interest that has come of late is to allow people to stretch their consciousness realms to a parameter where they can perhaps see that, if these aspects can link in one way or another to themselves, then they themselves must -it's a two-way street. Part of them must link back to those aspects inter-dimensionally.

Commander X's Guide to Incredible Conspiracies

Q: Where exactly are these beings coming from?

O'BRIEN: There's many beings coming from many different universes, many different galaxies. Which, again, is really an expression of the critical point that Earth is at right now, where we can make a difference to the evolution of All That Is.

Q: Now, you mentioned to me previously that you had worked with some people who had had abduction experiences and who had these implants placed in them. Which to a lot of these people seems to be a very frightening experience. What is your take on this? Why, if these beings that are coming here are so benevolent, why are they in a sense performing medical experiments and things that some people would consider very torturous?

O'BRIEN: Again, the initial impression is often highly fear-based and very torturous. However, as we as a species take back our power, and in delving into these experiences to allow people to remember or call forth the memories, there have always been contracts that they made with these species as to why they would undergo these experiences. It's never been quite the victim scenario that we would like to think. Once those contracts are understood, they can then as a human being take back their own power.

There's always a link that they can provide that allows themselves not only to transmute and ascend from the state of fear and the state of "victim-hood" but also allows that inter-species link to move on to its next higher evolutionary patterning level. As soon as we, within our own realm of experience, "get" that we no longer have to play out the galactic wars or even the wars within our own self-the "reactiveness" within ourselves, in our relationships, what we find is that things can be moved back into the state of the fact that All Exists and we don't need to play out the different polarities to know that these "existences" actually happen and are in perfect balance on a greater whole.

Q: What would you say is the next step for humankind in our evolution? And what is the ultimate totality or finality of all of this? Are the planet and the people on it transformed into some higher heavenly realm? Or what exactly is the conclusion we hear so much from the prophets about the coming of the Millennium? Is there to be a major event that will kind of shove this in our faces, so to speak?

O'BRIEN: What's actually happening is people's perceptions are almost being turned inside out. And as their perceptions and their consciousness are undergoing this dramatic shift, then the Earth no longer has to respond in quite the same ways that it has been. And the Earth herself can move to a higher evolutionary level – or a higher vibrational level. As to what that looks like, there is as many different realities for that possibility as there are people. The overall perspective is that a greater sense of unity and unification will prevail. But I have no prophecies. Depending on the consciousness that we as a people, and linking in with other species, what we hold will indeed create our reality.

So, one of the things that I forgot to mention about the grid is that we are the grid. As we affect and we change the vibrations in our own beingness, within our own body, we can affect the grid or this consciousness network that lies around the planet. In other words, if we're looking at trying to put out old belief systems and raise our vibration to be able to hold more love or light- it's akin to changing ourselves from a 50 watt light bulb to a 1000 watt light bulb. And as we become that 1000-watt light bulb, we work in harmony with the grid because we can connect up to those vibrations. So, therefore, it's something where we have an experience. The other thing about the grid is that it's foolproof as in you can't fool it. You can't say, "Okay, I'm going to try and do such and such" and then have greedy ulterior motives behind it. Greed is a vibration, and so you won't be able to link in and utilize that network of consciousness.

Q: You speak of this grid as if it were a living thing. Is it a living thing that was planted in the Earth? Or is it a computerized system? What exactly is it? Is it there in a physical sense somewhere? Could we dig it up? Or travel to the center of the Earth and find it?

O'BRIEN: No, it's an energetic link. It is an electromagnetic link. There is a number of different creative forces that exist. And they all link in concert with the grid. So, light will link with the grid. Sound will connect with the grid. Electromagnetics will link with the grid. Like I said, it's a nervous system. You can't really see it, yet it's a transmitter system or a communications system that allows interconnectedness or inter-relatedness.

The expression that you said-as a living, breathing thing-is also true in a larger sense. Because as we evolve through our beingness, through our energetics, and as we integrate more and more energetics, some of the old structures that were part of the grid will change and will evolve. For example, this trip to Alaska was to open a vortex that was one of twelve.

Some of the others that I worked with were in Indonesia and Hawaii, that actually in a sense held some of the old patternings, or old structures that allowed us to play out duality, to play out the expression of the belief that Creation manifests itself through polarity. But Creation already exists, that's what we're coming to understand.

Q: So was this planet that we live on then created by a God with this grid system in mind? Where does it date back? What is the evolution of the grid and of the planet?

O'BRIEN: The grid relates back to energetics. Which are movement patterns from which Creation is manifested. And in coming into form, there is -how can I explain? There are certain levels of frequency bands that are manifesting Creation. And the gird pattern is ilmost like a structure that holds the Forrnless expressions of Creation, that which we can't see, in some semblance or some framework that allows us to move within an evolutionary patterning, that there's an interconnectedness yet here is still a semblance of order as things are progressing and evolving.

Q: Now one of the things that we certainly have studied, or at least I have, is the beliefs of the Native-American shamans as well as shamans from different parts of the planet - they seem to have a certain respect for the globe that as been diminished by humankind in recent years. Were they in their own way "on' to the existence of this grid system?

O'BRIEN: In some ways, yes. Again, there are different expressions and different archetypes. The definition a shaman is one who follows or moves energy. So they would be quite apt to be aware of this sort of consciousness and how it can move as an interrelated or interconnected superstructure, you want to call it that. Whereas, you might have others who are from the same tribe whose focus was as a warrior. And they would probably not be aware of that, unless other tribal members were teaching it to them.

Q: Now, on this trip to Alaska, I noticed that you were particularly enthusiastic if not downright excited about going out and seeing the whales. What was the purpose of that and what did you accomplish? Because I know we did see quite a few of them, in fact, and I understand more so than usual.

O'BRIEN: The whales, as I mentioned earlier, were almost like what we would talk about as the higher beings or some of those beings of higher consciousness that we have-whether you want to call them "custodial gods" or "expressions of The Great White Brotherhood." We have many different expressions for higher beings that exist. And my knowingness is that the whales were using the same methods or working with the same sort of energy patterns and assisting us from below – that they are facilitating our next evolutionary jump as humankind. They're the ones that are saying that we as humans have the ability to connect it. And until we do, none of the rest of it gets connected.

Q: When you say they "say" are they saying this to you? Are you actually communicating with them?

O'BRIEN: I had the gift and the privilege of working in Australia a number of years back well, I would probably say the whales were working with me. I was out on a research vessel in Harvey Bay, Australia. And I had the opportunity, as we were looking at the effect of boat traffic on the whales as a research project, to study them at some length. At that time I had a situation, like a once in a lifetime thing, where I was actually in the water and had two very old whales, a male and a female, approach me. And there was total communication. There was total openness.

Elan says that other species such as the whales are crying out for help. Pollution has even caused them to change their migration habits. On our trip to Alaska, Elan attempted telepathic communication with several whales that came close to our vessel.

●   ●   ●

Saving Our Planet -World Peace Crystals Placed at North Pole.
By William Lee Rand

A cold wind whipped across the gravel runway as I walked from the plane to the small airport terminal at Resolute in Canada's Northwest Territory. It had taken two days to get here after teaching a Karuna class in New York City, yet I still had over eight hours of flight time left before I would get to my destination-the North Pole, where I planned to place a specially created crystal grid dedicated to world peace.

The terminal was filled with activity. A women's relay team, which was cross-country skiing to the Pole, was exchanging team members-one team arriving and one leaving. As I spoke to our organizer, I noticed that although I did not feel weak and my mind was clear, my vision and hearing were phasing in and out going from normal to almost black then back to normal. I realized that my system was attempting to adjust to the unusually high vibration of the area. At this latitude and time of year, the sun is always up and simply circles around a little above the horizon 24 hours a day. This combined with clear skies most of the time, blazing white snow and it's proximity to the North Pole, created an environment filled with intensity.

The temperature ranged from 10 degrees above to 10 degrees below zero F. which is not that cold, but with the wind chill, it can get much colder. The remainder of the journey would be in a "Twin Otten" a very rugged and powerful plane known as the "workhorse of the Arctic." It is equipped with retractable skis so it can land on both gravel runways (which is all they can have up here because of the permafrost) and snow or ice. Because good weather is important in order to land on the ice at the Pole, our departure time could change at a moment's notice. My ride up to the North Pole was possible because of an extra seat on the plane that would pick up a dog sled and cross-country ski team that was going there. Although we were scheduled to leave the next afternoon, a sudden change in weather put us on the plane in the early morning.

We stopped at the Eureka weather station on Ellesmere Island to refuel, then had to stay overnight as the weather changed again. We continued on the next day and landing on the Arctic ice, picked up the dog sled team, loading the dog sled, and dogs onto the plane along with the team members and proceeded on. The team had not made it to the Pole, so we were going to fly the remainder of the distance and land there. However, when we got over the Pole, it was covered with fog and the pilot could not see the ice clearly enough to land, so we circled and came back.

Not having placed the "Grid" at the Pole, I was disappointed and not sure what to do. So I made a call to the Center asking people to send Reiki energy to help the project, then I talked to the flight dispatcher to see if I could get on another flight.

There are actually two North Poles, one is geographic and one is magnetic. I chose the geographic pole simply because this was the pole I was offered a ride to, but then we were unable to land. I did not know there were flights to the magnetic pole even though I knew this would be the best place for the 'Grid.' After Reiki had been sent, the situation changed.

The flight dispatcher, being sympathetic to our cause, convinced the people going to pick up a Frenchman who was walking to the magnetic North Pole to allow me to go along on the flight. The magnetic North Pole is near Ellef Ringnes Island. After landing, I walked out away from the plane on sea ice. There I dedicated the World Peace Crystal Grid and gave it a final charging of Reiki. A picture was taken as it lay on the snow at the magnetic North Pole, copies of which are now available. A video was also made; then it was buried under the snow. When the sea ice melts in July, it will sink to the bottom of the ocean where it will remain forever.

The dedication was as follows: "I dedicate this World Peace Grid to create peace among all people on Earth. May all people realize that they come from the same source and because of this, may the members of all nations and all nationalities and the members of all religions and all spiritual paths and the members of all groups value and respect each other and work together to create peace among all people on Earth. May the founders of all religions and spiritual paths work together to create peace among all people on earth. May the followers of all religions and spiritual paths work together to create peace among all people on earth.

May all those who view this World Peace Grid be deeply healed and may they be empowered to create peace among all people on earth. I now place this World Peace Grid at the North Pole to remain forever creating and maintaining peace among all people on earth. So be it."

The World Peace Crystal Grid is made of solid copper in the shape of the heart chakra, 12 inches in diameter and plated with 24-carat gold. A 12-sided quartz pyramid is the center under which are inscribed the Usui power symbol and Karuna peace symbol. Double terminated quartz crystals are on each petal. Inscribed around the center are symbols for Goddess Religions all the world's religions and the words: "May the followers of all religions and spiritual paths work together to create peace among all people on earth."

The World Peace Crystal Grid is a tremendously powerful location. The magnetic energy of the earth flows through this area and continues to circulate all around the earth.

Commander X's Guide to Incredible Conspiracies

It is perhaps the strongest power spot in the world!

The Crystal Grid was placed on the snow at the magnetic North Pole to heal the earth. Inscribed under the crystal pyramid are the Reiki power symbol and the Karuna peace symbol circled by symbols of all major religions and independent spiritual paths, goddess, native people, etc.

When the World Peace Crystal Grid was made for the North Pole, one was also planned for the South Pole and two 12 sided crystals were cut from the same tabular crystal for use at the center of each grid. Because the central crystals are cut from the same piece of quartz!

The grids for both Poles will be naturally attuned to each other. Plans for the South Pole are forming, but it is likely not to take place for another year or so. If we are to create peace on Earth, it will be important for us to take the time to really understand and appreciate all groups of people. This includes other nationalities, other religious and spiritual groups and groups of every kind.

If you are a Reiki practitioner, remember it is important that there be harmony between all Reiki people regardless of organization or lineage. The Grid can be used for this purpose as well.

The better all Reiki practitioners and masters work together in harmony to heal each other and the planet, the more successful we will be. We are at such a critical time in the history of the earth that if the human population is to survive and also to prosper, we need to truly value and respect each other.

Every person and every group of people on earth has something of value to contribute and until we realize this and really respect all groups of people, we will not be able to be at peace within ourselves or to create peace in the world. As harmony grows between some groups, it will be easier for others until the process is complete. Once there is peace among all people on earth, a tremendous time of prosperity and well-being will ensue not only for people, but for all living things.

SECRET SOCIETIES AND THE NEW WORLD ORDER

Skullduggery
By Timothy Guy

Elihu Yale, born near Boston, Massachusetts in 1649, was educated in London before going on to acquire a fortune from trade, mostly through the notorious British East India Company (who by the 1830s were forcing the Indian farmers to grow poppies for opium). Yale later made a series of donations to the Collegiate School in New Haven, Connecticut, and soon after, in 1718, the school was rechristened Yale College.

In 1776, Nathan Hale, along with three other Yale graduates, belonged to one of America's first intelligence operations. Established by George Washington during the Revolutionary War, the network of spies operated successfully throughout war. Hale was the only agent to be discovered by the British, and after speaking his famous last words - "I only regret that I have but one life to lose for my country" - he was hung as a spy at age of twenty-one. The relationship between Yale and the "Intelligence Community" has been unique ever since. Hale is considered America's first spy, and his statue still stands in front of CIA Headquarters in Langley, Virginia...

In December of 1776, five students at William and Mary College founded a secret society. They called it Phi Beta Kappa. Its purpose was for the "promotion of literature and friendly intercourse among scholars." Its Latin motto translated as "Love of Wisdom, the Guide of Life." This original Phi Beta Kappa Society is considered to be the parent of all the Greek letter fraternities in America's collegiate system.

The Society has remained active ever since, except for a brief period during the Revolutionary War, when the approach of the British Army under General Cornwallis forced the college to close. After the war, the Phi Beta Kappa Society voted on a charter for branches at other colleges, and in 1780, a second chapter was created at Yale, and in 1781, a third branch opened at Harvard.

Secret societies have always been looked upon in a bad light, however, and in the early 1800s; pressure eventually forced all of the collegiate societies to go public. For Yale, the Oath of Secrecy was disregarded in 1831...

The secretary of Yales' Phi Beta Kappa chapter at the time the secrecy oath was disregarded was William Russell, a Yale junior and future class valedictorian. He came from a wealthy family (whose Russell & Company fortune was acquired through the trade mandated by the Opium Wars, whereby Britain forced the Chinese to import opium that the East India Company was forcing the Indians to grow). In 1832, the year after Phi Beta Kappa had been forced to go public, Russell and fourteen other students founded "The Order of Skull and Bones."

Researchers believe that the original reason behind the formation of the Skull and Bones was the desire simply to go against public pressure and recreate a secret society. A glance into their future would show this Order going beyond this goal and achieving far greater accomplishments.

The Order of the Skull and Bones. It is a club for seniors only. Each year fifteen Yale juniors are "tapped" by seniors to be initiated into next year's group. A member walks up, taps you on the shoulder and says: "Skull and Bones, accept or reject." You answer right then and there. And despite its shadowy reputation, its allure is apparent, for it has been observed that the group is geared more toward the success of its members in the post-collegiate world than in any philanthropic ideas.

Bones is a group of young men from affluent, well-established East Coast families, "literally a chosen elite," who are educated and prepared for positions of influence and power.

The Bonesmen hold their meetings each Thursday and Sunday on Yale campus. Since 1856, the meetings have been held in the "tomb," a vine-covered, windowless, mausoleum that sits on Yale campus where they still meet to this day. Unlike members of other societies, Bonesmen pay no dues. The land the mausoleum sits upon is owned by the Russell Trust Association, the Skull and Bones corporate shell, which owns nearly all of Yale University's real estate, as well as most of the land in Connecticut.

Members who have spoken about these secret meetings say: "It's a human bonding experience." "It isn't easy to keep one's guard up." "It's easy to let one's guard down." "The one thing we all agreed upon was that whatever was said at those meetings would never leave the room."

Outside researchers have long observed: "Connections are power. It means something to have access to the sort of network that a member of Skull and Bones can tap." "They are one extended family." "In the Skull and Bones they all stand together. It is the greatest allegiance in the world."

The benefit of belonging to the Skull and Bones is the networking. You get to meet wealthy and influential people whom you otherwise wouldn't meet. They are your brother Bones. Since its founding, the Skull and Bones has inducted over twenty-five hundred members. At any given time, an estimated seven hundred of those members are living. When one considers the list of prominent members of Skull and Bones, living and dead, the true extent of their network of connections begins to come to light.

The Order of Skull and Bones has been a recruiting ground for young men destined for success in influential sectors of American life. Bonesmen are automatically offered jobs upon graduation at firms and organizations owned by fellow brothers, and as a result, the Skull and Bones has had a voting hand in virtually every industry from financial institutions to railroads to oil companies and Wall Street law firms.

Its tentacles of influence reach most notably into the CIA, an organization which apparently has the make-up of a Yale class reunion. This is the Intelligence connection that goes back to the spy Nathan Hale and the Revolutionary War.

The Skull and Bones has enormous influence upon the Federal Reserve System (which is "neither federal nor has any reserves") but rather is a cartel of private banks that controls the American economy, thereby controlling the destiny of every American. Bonesmen also form the nucleus of the privately run Council on Foreign Affairs, and the Trilateral Commission, both of whom are guiding forces behind the drive towards global unification - a One World Government.

Many observers believe that this plan for a One World Government was hatched and the seed planted long ago. The very seal of the United States, as seen on the American dollar bill, has two Latin phrases surrounding the All-Seeing Eye, translating roughly as "Announcing the Birth - A New Order of Ages."

The New World Order idea is an old one. The Skull and Bones supposedly developed it from the Hegelian theory, where you play one extreme against the other. Take one force (thesis) and bring it into conflict with another force (anti-thesis), and you will create a third force (synthesis). Hegel was talking, of course, of the spiritual and not of the material, but for Bonesmen, capitalism versus socialism could result in a New World Order.

One would first have to demonstrate that a One World Government was the best option for peace and stability. This might not be such a hard sell, especially if one considers and can capitalize on the threat of global terrorism. The average citizen might want the special security of the single All-Seeing Eye looking out for them.

It would mean a world where the State would take over an individual's rights for the good of the whole. Individual freedom would be entrusted into the hands of a small ruling elite. A microchip could be installed beneath your skin so you could buy and sell without cash, and you could always be located, for your own safety.

A One World Government would mean a central world banking system and one currency. It will mean a one-world army under one military authority. And, of course, there will be a microchipped population connected to a global computer. There is already such a computer in existence, located in Belgium, serving the European Union. It is known as the B.E.A.S.T (Belgium Electronic Account Surveillance Team). The Biblical Mark of the Beast will most likely be a microchip, embedded in one's skin, and wired to a central computer. Big Brother won't be watching you. Big Brother will be you.

The U.S. military is already implanting microchips in their new recruits to act as a means of identification. The nation is gearing up for all pets to be implanted with microchips. Can microchipping for the average citizen be far behind?

The idea of being dominated by an Orwellian global computer can seem at the same time so improbable and yet so terrifying that Karl Marx probably put it best when he said that thirst is the thesis, beer is the antithesis, and Synthesis is under the table.

Bonesmen have occupied practically every political office from the Presidency of the United States (three times) to Senators and Governors and cabinet officials. President George H. W. Bush (Bones '48), in a speech to Congress in 1990, said, "Out of these troubled times, our fifth objective - a new world order - can emerge." His son, President George W. Bush (Bones '68) wrote in his autobiography in 1999: "My senior year I joined Skull and Bones, a secret society, so secret I can't say anything more."

The Bush lineage is an impressive one. George W.'s grandfather was Prescott Bush (Bones '17), an "investment banker" who acquired a fortune making investments for the Nazis. In "George Bush: The Unauthorized Biography" the authors (W. Tarpley and A. Chaitkin) write: "It's a matter of record that the property of Prescott Bush was seized (Vesting Order Number 248 - 11/17/42) under the Trading with Enemy Act. Prescott Bush and the other directors of the Union Banking Corporation were declared legally 'front men for the Nazis.'"

Prescott Bush went on to become a U.S. Senator and married into the powerful Walker family, also "investment bankers." Prescott's father-in-law was George Herbert Walker, who wasn't a Bonesman himself, but had a Bones son, George Herbert Walker, Jr. (Bones '27), co-founder of the Mets, and eventually a Bones grandson - George Herbert Walker III (Bones '53). This lineage would also include George Herbert Walker Bush (U.S. President, 1989-1993), and his son, George Walker Bush (U.S. President (2001-present).

In fact, the last three U.S. Presidents have all held Yale degrees: George H.W. Bush, Bill Clinton (who holds a Yale law degree but no membership in the Skull and Bones) and George Walker Bush. In the 2000 presidential elections, three out of four names on the Republican and Democratic ticket were Yale students: George W. Bush and his Vice President Dick Cheney (who withdrew from Yale before graduation), and Senator Joseph Lieberman, who ran as vice president with Al Gore (Harvard).

In the 2004 elections, we will have the first-ever Bones versus Bones presidential race, with three out of the four names on the tickets being Yale grads. The two fellow Bonesmen going head to head are George Bush and Senator John Forbes Kerry (Bones '66). Not only is Kerry a Bonesman, but his wife Theresa Heinz Kerry, was once married to Senator John Heinz (Bones '31), of Heinz ketchup fame. Look out Hilary fans. She is a Yale graduate too.

It looks to a fine example of American's one-party state when it doesn't matter which candidate is elected president of the United States, because the same elite will be in power. We have no choice. Since both men are sworn Bonesmen, will it make any difference in the foreign and domestic policies of the United States which man wins the November 2004 election?

The more secretive a society is allowed to become, the more powerful it can grow. Quietly it can work its tentacles into far-reaching spaces. Power can be insidious if allowed to creep into positions of high authority unnoticed. It is the nature of man to be greedy, and the more powerful one becomes, the greedier one can be, and absolute power corrupts, absolutely.

(Witness the East India Company, the Opium Wars, and the Nazi regime.) One researcher calls the Skull and Bones "An international Mafia - unregulated and all but unknown."

Perhaps it is hard to believe in the suggested power and influence of the Skull and Bones because on the surface such a grand scheme would seem so implausible. And the rumors do run vast and deep about the Skull and Bones. Consider the myth that a Bonesman is required to leave the room whenever a non-member mentions the name of his society. It makes the whole thing seem like a lunatic conspiracy. And equally outrageous are any plans for global domination. Again, our scoffing would help keep their secrecy in tact.

The Order of the Skull and Bones has been called the most powerful secret society the United States has ever known. Its members are called knights, and the rest of us are perhaps pawns in their chess game.

The inscription on the Skull & Bones "tomb" reads: Who was the fool, who the wise man, beggar or king? Whether poor or rich, all's the same in death.

I include that quote only because it may be relative to our investigation. And why not hold your secret meetings in a "tomb?" A mausoleum will make one-half of the population very fearful, while the other half will be laughing in ridicule at such a preposterous tale...

Postscripts:

The Order of Skull and Bones was exclusively male until the 1990s, when the members voted to admit women.

President George W. Bush's daughter Barbara is rumored to have been "tapped" her junior year at Yale but turned them down to join another society. With such a lustrous lineage full of Bonesmen, she apparently doesn't need Skull and Bones connections.

Skull and Bones' original name before being changed was "The Order of Scull and Bones," a scull being a quick, gliding boat, probably a reference to a sport of rowing that was in vogue at the time. The Rowing Crew at Yale, established in 1843, was America's first collegiate sports team.

The year 2001 saw Yale's three-hundredth anniversary. Their official seal includes the Hebrew words Urim and Thummim, commonly translated as Light and Truth. Yales' endowment for the year 2001 was $10.7 billion dollars, an increase from the previous year's $10.1 billion.

The Phi Beta Kappa Society is still active today, with a living membership numbering more than 500,000. It is America's oldest college fraternity.

Timothy Guy is the author of *Aliens Over America: Twelve Fantastic Books Reviewed Including Interviews With Authors*. Timothy Beckley has called the book "one of the greatest UFO conspiracy books I have ever read." The book covers alien topics from Dr. Frank Stranges to Time Travel to Tim Beckley. To order *Aliens Over America*, contact this publisher, or for an autographed copy, send $25.00 to AOA Press. P.O. Box 572377, Tarzana, CA 91357.

●   ●   ●

The Crescent and the Swastika?
By Juan Carlos Mallory (Thanks to Scott Corales)

In 2003, readers and TV viewers across Spain were stunned by a spectacular and deadly achievement: Antonio Salas (pseudonym employed by a well-known member of Spain's media establishment) had done the seemingly impossible by infiltrating his country's growing Neo-Nazi subculture and capturing it all on videotape.

The impressive, damning footage was aired on TV and the magnitude of the skinhead movement, its convoluted ideology, and its seemingly endless recruiting pool became known to public at large. Salas delivered the coup de grace with a book, Diario de un Skin (Diary of a Skinhead), which recounts the author's year-long odyssey to join the ranks of the Neo-Nazi movement through the Internet and finally his physical immersion into the subculture, with its attendant perils.

The Neofascist movement is spreading apace not only throughout the Iberian Peninsula but through the rest of Europe, a situation discussed in a number of periodicals and books. But one of the most interesting revelations made by the author did not involve the cradle of Western civilization; rather, it concerned the spread of fascist thought throughout the Islamic World.

A number of Spanish Neofascist publications, particularly one entitled Resistencia (Resistance), had quoted Adolf Hitler's belief that 1930's Germany was closer ideologically to the Islamic nations of the world than it was to its fellow European countries, primarily due to their hatred of "the Jewish enemy." Inspired by this belief, budding skinheads have found solace in the speeches of the late Ayatollah Ruhollah Khomeini, whose speeches and those of Hitler "appear to have issued from the same person", according to the publication.

Other reactionary publications that Salas encountered during his circumnavigation of the Skinhead world was one entitled Handschar, a word describing a certain type of bladed weapon. This islamic-fascist publication juxtaposed Nazi emblems such as the ubiquitous swastika with the Islamic crescent moon or the scimitar, featuring photographs of Arab volunteers who fought alongside the SS, tracts on Hitler's pro-Muslim policy and "ethnic cleansing" in the Caucasus, and images of the best-known Islamic Nazi: Hajj Amin Husseini.

An Unlikely Alliance

Born in Jerusalem in 1893 during the dying days of the Ottoman Empire, Husseini served in the Sultan's army during World War I and saw the Turkish realm defeated on all sides and dismembered by the victorious European powers. Ascending to the rank of Grand Mufti of Jerusalem in 1921 as Palestine became a British mandate under the League of Nations, he voiced the collective fear that Jewish immigration to Transjordan would be harmful to the Arab cause, and masterminded many anti-Jewish efforts and riots throughout the 1920's and '30s.

When war broke out in Europe in 1939, Nazi Germany found a ready ally in Husseini, who probably felt that such an alliance would be beneficial to his political dreams, since it was likely that the Germans would win the war and reward their supporters handsomely. It was also true that Husseini found an ideological kinship between Nazism and Islam, to the extent of requesting that the German High Command apply the "Final Solution" to the Jewish communities of North Africa and Transjordan, and even that the Luftwaffe bombard Tel Aviv – much as it had done in Guernica. Husseini had already called for a Jihad against the British in 1941, to no effect. The German offensive in Iraq in 1941 had been a dismal failure, and Raschid al-Ghailani, the Iraqi chancellor – another Hitler sympathizer – was forced to flee to Iran.

"The Arabs are Germany's natural allies," said Husseini in a speech delivered in November 1941 before the Antikomintern Pact conference, "because they have the same common foes: the British, the Jews and the Communists. They are therefore willing to collaborate cordially with Germany and enter into war on its side, and not only from a point of view we could consider negative, by carrying out acts of sabotage and promoting revolts, but positively as well, creating an Arab Legion. As allies, the Arabs might prove more useful to Germany than it might appear at first glance..." (Paul Schmidt, Hitler's Interpreter, London 1950).

Husseini's sympathies for Hitler did not avail him in the end either. The British beat Rommel out of Africa and any hope of a Nazi occupation of Palestine was gone; at the war's end, Husseini fled to France and later to Egypt, despite numerous extradition requests by European countries (particularly Yugoslavia, since Husseini had played a major role in recruiting and bankrolling Muslim fighters in Bosnia who killed many of Tito's partisans). This controversial figure died in Beirut in 1974.

Husseini remains the brightest light in the Islamic-Fascist firmament, but not to all. A Palestinian website makes the following statement: "What makes many Palestinians extremely angry is that the memories of the Holocaust are being exploited to paint Palestinians as Nazis. Such dangerous comparisons and propaganda tactics are continuously fed to many Israeli and Jewish school children [...] especially upon visiting the Holocaust museum at Yad Vahsem. It should be emphasized that many life-size pictures of al-Hajj Amin standing alongside Hitler are on display at Yad Vashem. It is

hypocritical to hold Palestinians responsible for the "ill-fated" choice of al-Hajj Amin, while Israelis and Jews still blind themselves to the choices some of their leaders made during WW II."
(www.palestineremembered.com/Acre/Palestine-Remembered/Story420.html)

The Palestinian leader was not the Third Reich's only ally in the Middle East: according to José Miguel Romaña, author of Nazismo Esoterico: Iraq, Syria and Iran boasted Nazi sympathizers and abetted the operations of the Reich's agents in a manner reminiscent of how the fictional Nazis of Spielberg and Lucas's Raiders of the Lost Ark conducted operations in the Middle East. These close ties had been carefully cultivated by Germany during the previous century. During a state visit to Damascus in November 1898, Kaiser Wilhelm II spoke the following words to Abdul Hamid II, the Turkish Sultan: "His Majesty the Sultan, as well as the three hundred million Mohammedans who venerate the caliph's presence in him, can be sure that the German emperor shall always be their friend."

German occultists also developed their own relationships with the Middle East. Rudolph von Sebottendorff, founder of the Thule Gessellschaft, was initiated into the Muslim brotherhood known as the Bekashi, whose members believed in the quest for the "Philosopher's Stone" which had been the goal of European alchemists of the Renaissance.

This initiation prompted Von Sebottendorff to write: "Islam is not a petrified religion. On the contrary, its vitality is greater than that of Christianity. Where can its strength come from? From its occult roots, from a living water which fertilized the early Church and which caused the most beautiful flowers to bloom in the Middle Ages..."

But as undercover journalist Antonio Salas would discover over fifty years later, these points and counterpoints had little meaning to Spanish Neofascists: some of them have gone as far as to accept religious instruction at madrassas and make the pilgrimage to Mecca. College professor José Rios Camacho embraced Islam and became Suman Hanza; other newsletters and fanzines espousing Islamic Nazism appeared, calling for closer ties with Muslim fundamentalists in the struggle against the "corrupt, Zionist-controlled West". Salas himself is moved to say: "We are therefore witnessing a solid fusion between Neo-Nazi ideologues and the Islamic world, not just merely distant, purely diplomatic cooperation."

Another Spanish journalist, Tomás Navarro, has observed that some of the supporters of Islamic Nazism have gone as far as to suggest that their enclaves should "disconnect" from the rest of society and even go as far as minting their own coinage in an effort break with the dollar, the ultimate "Zionist" currency.

A Desperate Flight, or Flight of Fancy?

Fallen leaders often create a vortex of confusion when they fall. It will suffice to watch any evening news broadcast to see the turmoil that exists in Iraq in 2003 in the wake of Saddam Hussein's defeat and prior to his ignominious capture, some argued that the Iraqi strongman had not died or gone into hiding, but that he was alive and well "somewhere".

A similar situation existed nearly sixty years ago, when the Stockholm-based "Free German Press Service" ran the story that Adolf Hitler had not committed suicide in his Berlin bunker and that the remains found by advancing Soviet troops had been those

Commander X's Guide to Incredible Conspiracies

of the Fuhrer's "double", August Bartholdi. The fact that many Nazi ideologues and collaborators had managed to escape to South America and other parts of the world led many to believe in the possibility that the German strongman had also made good his escape to parts unknown.

Much has been made of the Third Reich's fascination with the Orient, and more than one book has been written about Hitler's fascination with Eastern mysticism. *Planéte*, the controversial '70s French publication of the occult, ran an article regarding the "Fuhrer's alleged last flight" aboard a He 277 VI heavy bomber on April 30, 1945 to an unknown destination Central Asia. According to the flight plan appearing in the August 1969 issue of the magazine, the He 277 had a range of nearly 6000 kilometers at 490 KMH, which could have easily brought it to any airfield in that part of the world. Still others suggest that the aircraft would have been forced to stop to refuel somewhere, perhaps Damascus or Baghdad. And what was this "ultimate destination"?

The magazine suggests either Afghanistan or the Tibetan Plateau, perhaps in a desperate mission to contact the "dark adepts" who had allegedly smiled on the Nazis only twelve years earlier. It is a matter of historical record that the Nazis sent expeditions to the Far East on an almost yearly basis, leading to the creation of the oft-discussed "Order of Green Men" who allegedly helped the Reich employ sorcery during the World War II. If the He 277 VI's mission was indeed to reach Tibet, there is no further evidence of its fate. It is almost certain that Communist Chinese forces would have made mention of German operatives in that part of the world after their brutal takeover of Tibet, but the record is strangely silent. If the long-range bomber went to Afghanistan, where did it go? Did its crew seek entrances to the fabled "inner earth" and the lost realm of Agartha, or did they merely become hopelessly lost in the maze of caves such as the ones at Tora Bora which acquired notoriety in late 2001, during the efforts to capture Osama Bin Laden?

And what if we dare take a complete leap into fantasy, away from the meager source documents at our disposal? Could the Nazis have made contact not with any eldritch realm, but with very real Muslim secret societies, descendants of the legendary Hashashin or Assassins, who pledged their aid to the doomed Reich's cause? Could the rise of fascism in the Muslim world stem from seeds planted so long ago?

An Answer in Prophecy?

Argentinean novelist Hugo Wast made an effort to study and interpret the ***Book of Revelation*** (or the Apocalypse) in the early years of the 20th century. He was fascinated by the concept of the Biblical "seven-headed Beast", which has been characterized by some as representing the "heads" of the main European powers. Wast came up with a disturbing and new possibility.

According to his book ***El Sexto Sello*** ("The Sixth Seal"), the seven heads of the beast are seven countries. Of these seven, five had already vanished by the time St. John composed the Book of Revelation in the 1st century A.D.: these would have been the Egyptians, Assyrians, Medes, Persians and Greeks. The sixth head still existed at the time that John received his fearsome visions – the mighty Roman Empire.

But the prophet hastens to add that when the seventh head arrives, it is necessary that its duration be brief. Wast interprets this final head of the Biblical beast to represent Islam, which arrived in the 7th century A.D. and became a world power in the 15th century, withering in importance shortly thereafter.

The Argentinean novelist attaches great significance to the cryptic passage in Rev. 13:3 which reads: "And I saw one of his heads as it were wounded to death, and his deadly wound was healed; and all the world wondered after the beast". Wast then asks his reader the following question: "What empire could this be, that almost dead toward the end of times, is reborn by the power of the dragon? None of the first five, which were long gone in St. John's day, nor the Roman Empire, which was not only wounded but which vanished altogether, as history shows us."

Wast now moves in for the prophetic kill: "We can interpret the prophecy to mean Islam, which appeared politically wounded to death after 1918 but which now, like a lion who has slept for centuries on the shifting sands of its deserts, sends out the signal of its impending awakening."

So far, so good. But what evidence do we have that this prophecy follows the interpretation given to it? The analyst now summons the heavy artillery provided by ancient numerical magic. Since scriptural sources insist that the "beast" will coincide with the also-prophesied "Antichrist", discovering the numerical value of one will doubtlessly provide the identity of the other: this brings into play the ominous number "666", which has been overused by authors of paranormal fiction.

Wast insists that the name Muhammad, written in Greek, spells out "666": "History forgot an interpretation which today regains its importance in the light of contemporary events. If the first Muhammad wasn't the Antichrist, and if Muhammad II (the Turkish sultan) wasn't the Antichrist either, there could very well be a Muhammad III, lord of Asia and half of Africa, with hundreds of millions of subjects."

One shudders to think that this new Sultan of the East could be Hitler with a turban...

Scott Corrales is a writer and translator of UFO and paranormal subjects in Latin America and Spain. Scott edits *Inexplicata: The Journal of Hispanic Ufology*.
lornis1@juno.com

The Suppressive Force
By Susan Reed

Introduction

Here are transcripts of conversations I had in November 2003 with a man who was a member of what he termed "the Suppressive force" also called the "illuminati" or the "global elite". I am making this information public for my protection, as they don't harm those who go public, as it will add credibility to the information. I believe the information to be true. I will first say that Steve is a junior in their organization that is the reason for some of the errors that he has made where I am concerned.

I discovered who Steve was by accident in May 2002. I was his girlfriend, we had fallen out and he fired weapon number 2 (see weapons) at me from a distance. He does this routinely in his personal life to get back at any slight done to him. This time he was found out. I am more sensitive than most and instantly knew that he was responsible. I confronted him and he panicked and used weapon number 1 on me. Steve was 20 miles away at the time! I ended up a hospital and almost died.

Thinking that I was going to die he told me he worked for a suppressive force and that looked at from a higher perspective bad is OK, three neighbors had taken me to hospital and I had told them that Steve was responsible. When he found this out and to this day I do not know how he did it, he removed the effects of the weapon. I have always admired him for "saving me" although his motives were keeping himself out of jail. We continued to see each other; I am not great at picking men. Unpleasant, mistreatment is the norm for me.

I did not want to go public with this information but I have to stop Steve. He has been trying to harm me for months since we split up so that I would loose my credibility or shut me up for good. His ego blinds him and he has to win. I have even had to make a Will last December with instructions to publicize all my information in the event of my death or disappearance. The information on the Greys and NASA has resulted in me going on their death list. I know their ways and I recorded the conversations to protect myself in the event that we finished our relationship. Soon afterwards we did.

When we split up he pursued me out of Spain using a colleague in Leon, then out of a good job in Rochfield, England, again using a colleague there. I had not told a soul about what I knew for 18 months nor had I any desire to do so.

I am not interested in conspiracies and would much rather be advising on nutrition. I knew that could stop him by going public but I didn't want to do it. Instead I just kept avoiding them by moving at considerable cost to myself. I had pleaded with him on the phone, but he wouldn't stop. I sought refuge in America and he even got a colleague near Middletown, California to find me and then harm me. I had nowhere else to go and backed in a corner I told him that I would go to the Spanish Press with who he really was unless he stopped, He did. Just the threat of this exposure was enough to have Steve transferred out of Spain this January where he had settled for two years to I think Germany.

The suppressive force is a secret organization that is taking control of the planet without us knowing about it. They place themselves in positions of power and they are also found in all walks of life and there is a ground force covering geographical areas and this was Steve's role. His area used to be the Costa del sol, Andalusia, Spain that he called his "turf" He lived on the road to Mijas. Steve termed his organization the Suppressive Force because they are using techniques to suppress us all so that we don't realize what is going on and so we are too caught up in our problems to even care. Suppression would mean suppressing our intellect as described under nutrition, suppressing our abundance as described under debt, suppressing our health as described under virus's and nutrition and the weapons that they use, suppressing our consciousness as described under anti-higher consciousness programme, art and architecture.

The transcripts take the form of conversations we had and I have also included evidence provided by my own experiences. I have not included all of my questions, which were probing to reduce down the size of the document. The man does swear a great deal socially so excuse the language.

About the man in question: There are no conspiracy or even political books in his house. He lives a façade. His persona is a jovial cockney (a term for a Londoner) a 42-year-old tall black man from Walthmonstow London. He has a hidden strength and wisdom that didn't fit with his persona. He has extraordinary mental abilities he was able to memorize long telephone numbers with ease.

He was an expert on the computer although he did not use this for his "day job". His thoughts are stronger and clearer than other peoples and I was able to pickup his thoughts although I am not telepathic. He even used advanced mental processes to seduce women, I know because he did them on me. His abilities extended to such things as remote viewing, astral projection and mind scanning. All these abilities he disguised even the way he spoke would change remarkably on the phone to work colleagues. Basically he was trying to disguise his real identity.

He is extremely knowledgeable on all subjects. His eyes have a steeliness about them that was unexpected. He avoids talking about himself and when he does it was always positive He was paranoid about other people being psychic; I believe he was frightened that they would discover who he was.

He is a Jekyll and Hyde Character both extremely harmful and helpful with a desire to harm and help. He was like two opposite people rolled into one. I was harmed and also given help. I found this very confusing.

He is extremely cruel and evidence I have is his cruelty towards me, we were going out and he kept me subjected to some of the weapons when he could have so easily stopped them. I accepted this behavior, a flaw in myself.

He openly displayed animal cruelty by cutting a ducks neck with a blunt knife and watching it slowly bleed to death for all to see. I am an animal lover and did what I could to help the poor animal.

He has amazing success with women. Remarkable considering he is not an attractive man, nor even the smooth charmer. He admires female beauty very much and his expectations in this area go far beyond his own attractiveness and yet all his girlfriends are very attractive. I was astonished.

I believe the reason for this is the seduction techniques he uses I experienced these seduction techniques and they involved advanced mental processes. I suddenly became very attracted to him and yet I was always tense around him. His womanizing was rampant, above anything or anyone else I knew had ever experienced before and his interests were only there until the women stayed the night and once this was achieved he completely lost interest.

One of his duties as odd as it may sound is the collection of DNA samples; mine were taken along with many of the women I knew. Once his initial seduction ends I found him to be negative about humanity, he hated the Spanish. He would constantly pull me down with phrases such as

"You're hopeless"; I was never any good at anything. He became a bully, unpleasant and critical and yet my attraction persisted.

Despite all the remarkable abilities that he had there are hidden ego problems that has resulted in this document being written. He has told me, "I've got an ego and it gets in my way. I push too far and don't let off when others would have saw reason. My feelings are...I want to get that bitch -- I want to squash her down -- I get blinded and can't see reason.

Q - This is my question. S - this is his answer.

Their overall plan

Q - Why are you here?
S - To take over the planet, girl. We are in control right now -we'll have you all under wraps
Q - How?
S - With an implant
Q - Is it a microchip?
S - Maybe, maybe not.
Q - What about that lens of the eye identity thing?
S - We want to do that - so we can identify you all - no fake passports, we'll know who you are.
Q - What is the implant?
S - It's a little device, a bit like a part to a computer - a few millimeters long.
Q - What's it made of?
S - Some kind of plastic and some metal and this and that.
Q - Are you using it already?
S - Yeah we've got a few people tagged up.
Q - Who?
S - Prisoners, yeah we've tried it on animals.
Q - How will people agree to this chip?
S - They'll want it, because they'll think it's a good thing
Q - Why?
S - Because we are rigging it right now - dinero (money) girl - it aint secure - theft, fraud, money laundering, wallets getting nabbed, credit card fraud, lost pins. A microchip will seem a better option - you'll be totally secure, no theft what so ever.
S - That's are second option init, our numero uno is the identity card , plan A and the identity card will replace everything - your passport, NHS number, drivers license and that's another way we can put the chip in, social security number, because they'll get lost and it will makes things awkward for you - no holiday abroad for the next year because there'll be delays in replacing it - if that's lost everything's gone hasn't it - they'll have no way of doing nothing until it's replaced and we'll probably say we'll replace it at a drop of a hat but then things will change and it aint going to be replaced so easy - extremely convenient after the deed. We may try both and see what works out.

Q - What are you doing with plan B.

S - We're rigging things right now.

Q - How?

S - Money ain't going to be money quite soon - the euro is part of it - mass facile (easier).

Q - What will happen to the euro?

S - It will lose its value to force you all in to it - then when everyone has got the euro there ain't going to be no euro - it will be all on your cards - no dinero at all.

Q - What will happen to the euro?

S - I ain't telling yeah - the euro will keep dropping to about 1.1euro per pound - so the euros strong so you'll want it.

S - There will be incentives (for no money) - maybe we'll just withdraw it all - then it is all on cards and then the card ain't no good, they ain't secure and you are going to want something different - because you'll get ripped off - credit card fraud - its all being set up right now.

Q - How?

S - No we don't need no fucking pin numbers for credit cards - if you have to give your pin then its secure isn't it - so we'll stop that, there will be no pin usage and we will make it easy to steal from you.

S - Yes I do credit card fraud - I'm encouraged to - on the computer - I purchase things on the computer using fake credit cards - well they are other peoples.

S - We can't do much with switch cards (it will be credit and switch together) other than make it difficult for you - its already happening - they get lost and they ain't replaced so quickly - they ain't secure, till receipts. Credit cards are the best for you, put you all in debt - then you are all going to be in debt and then we'll up the stakes, interest rates - they'll shoot up and then we'll come up with some better deal and you'll want it.

S - Credit cards are easy to come by and that's us and we're the credit cards, we make the rules and the rules are geared so you spend more than you earn, you're all in debt. We 're in control of most of the credit cards and they are fucking easy to come by.

S - We're trying to stop pins and anyone that opposes us gets it - we killed a geezer because he didn't support us - yeah he was in parliament and he snuffed it - heart attack - it was us - it was this year (2003) - our whirly thing (see weapons.) - during one of our meetings -early in the year- march - we'd been working on him before-his blood, making him more susceptible - it did not look natural, we take our chances. Our heart attacks are a bit different - because the bloke don't have no clot, no fucking ischaemia - we don't fucking allow an autopsy.

Q - Why?

S - Because they would find nothing wrong with him. It's always at the same fucking time of day, between two and three a.m. (By four a few geezers are getting up) normally at 2:40am is the exact time and we all work on people together.

S - If you had pins are plan would not work and we'd have to rethink.

S - Anyone with any sense would want pins at the till -and some countries use it and we 're going to stop it.

S - Tony Blair wants a fucking pin - the fucking shit rag.

S - Tony Blair ain't going to last long if he promotes pins.

Q - Credit card fraud- right now I get all the money back.

S - That will change, we'll stop all that, when you have no choice - when there's no dinero (money), we'll change the rules, maybe we'll pay a bit but not the full whack, the new rules are that you ain't going to get your money back if it's stolen - we just can't afford it - we'll reduce the time period down - 4hrs to report it or maybe we'll lower the amount.

Q - What about protection?

S - We'll try and make insurance protection hard to come by, lots of exclusions, things like that.

Q - How to avoid the microchip?

S - Get yourself out of society, don't pay your dues, no bank account - that's basically the main way of doing it.

Q - What do you want?

S - We want you planet, no two ways about it, that's all we want.

S - You are all going to snuff it one day and then are we'll take over and this is our planet not Yours.

Q - How are you going to kill us?

S - We'll have you all implanted and then we'll set this timer ticking and you'll all go off pot, the implant will wipe you all out

S - We'll rig it so it kills you - it will electrify you -we're not sure yet exactly how we are going to do it - no we can't use virus's it ain't effective - some sort of electrocution.

S - Right now we haven't got the technology- we are working on it.

Q - Are you destroying the Peruvian rainforest?

S - Yeah we are, we ain't in there so we've got to do a bit to harm them, haven't we. We ain't got Peru have we and if we were in there no rainforest would be touched but right now we've got to do it. We've got to get those natives out of Peru so we can get them civilized - we don't want no-one left who ain't chipped up. Natives who ain't civilized can't be part of our plan so we do what we can to destroy their culture and their habitat so they have to tow the line - we want them all to be under our thumb - they don't have no banks and that's the fucking problem isn't it - no banks means no microchip.

What Can We Do to Stop You?

S - If you all refuse or a lot of you refuse to take part in our control mechanisms then our plan won't work. You could all refuse to use credit cards and bank cards and then we ain't got a leg to stand on.

Q - What is the most important thing anyone could do to stop you and keep the planet to themselves?

S - Riot like crazy and that will do it. Refuse all credit cards. Campaign for a pin if you use credit cards. Refuse to send your children to school. Expose the top dogs. Refuse to vote for any president what so ever because it will always mean we're in control. Take all your money out of the bank and put it in a safe deposit box. Expose us basically and then we won't hang around. If you don't use a credit card then we ain't going to be able to do away with money and if money is still there we can't chip you and without a chip we can't destroy you. Right now there's still money around but when we need to withdraw money then you need to prevent us doing that by not wanting it and the way to do that is not use credit cards.

Q - How are you going to get rid of money?

S - It will seem more sensible to have everything on card

Q - Why?

S - It's going that way already. It's so easy to use a card why bother with money, there'll still be cheques, cheques or a card. The protests/ riots need to be when we propose getting rid of money, because once we've done that we're on a role - more and more stuff is on cards will simplify things.

Q - What will children use?

S - Children will have cards too- their parents, with a spending limit on it. At the till there won't be no cheques - it will all be on card. The shops won't accept anything but cards soon.

Q - Why?

S - Because it's easier. We have to remove money in gradual stages, so it's harder to use, cash machines ain't safe. People will start getting mugged at cash machines, the machine will swallow their card more easily, they've got no card for another 20 days, the banks are open at shit hours, you've got to take time off work to get there - huge queues at lunchtime. We'll make it a dam side harder to get your cash. They'll invent something else and it will seem like the ideal way of purchasing, like an identity card- it will give you everything you need in one card but then of course it will be converted to a chip because they'll get lost

Wars

S - Its not about the money, it's about getting into power and a bit more besides - keep the masses down and poor.

S - Iraq. We ain't got Iraq. We are working on that one. We'll use the U.S. and Great Britain to get Iraq for us. Other countries that we don't have, we'll start having wars so we can take control. We create wars so we can take control. We create wars because we have to, we'd rather not have them because they wreck the environment and they cost an arm and a leg. Wars help us get in power.

Other Members of the Suppressive Force - Naming Names

Q - Name some members of the suppressive force for me? What do you look like?

S - We want to look bog standard, normal, so no one suspects us of being anything other than who we portray. We never look like hippies it's the last thing we want to do.

S - Franklin Roosevelt.

Q - Why are your not always presidents.

S - Well we are sometimes but we prefer not to be in the spotlight, blame Bush and he ain't the reason.

Q - How bout a 4-year presidency?

S - Well it ain't long enough is it, a lot of work for just 4 years, we'd rather be in power longer and not be ousted, but it has been known. We are more behind the scenes and it's also because we don't want the finger pointed at us.

70 per cent of the U.S. government is us. We also control the media. We need them everywhere, certain films shouldn't be made. We promote certain types of movies, war, and violence. We try to stop new age films.

We don't want alien films made unless they are pure fantasy, Close Encounters of the Third Kind, that film we never wanted made. We don't want people thinking of aliens and UFOs except in a negative way.

Commander X's Guide to Incredible Conspiracies

Weapons

Weapon Number 1 is used to kill and it appears as though the victim has had a heart attack, always at night, time of death 2:40am or soon afterwards. This weapon has been used on me twice Once by Steve (see intro) and the second time by Steve's colleague and both times at 2:40am. Steve has told me that three or more of them fire this in unison to kill. In my case only one person used it on me. He has also told me that they use this weapon at night, as there is less interference.

This weapon constricted my chest to the point that I almost died. Evidence that Steve uses this weapon is that he would get up at this time several days a week and work on his computer. (He does not need to be near his victim) do this. He has told me that the best protection is to tell every one publicly that there is no problem with the heart and have it checked out by a doctor and keep home addresses unknown.

S - Its like a missile aimed at a certain point of your body - I tell the machine where you are and what part of your body

Q - How?

S - Via the computer (internet?) - I can't communicate with that machine telepathically, its got to be done via the computer. We don't always need to all get together, I type in your location in co-ordinates, once I've typed in the machine sends you that missile, its harmful energy, particles of energy that are vibrating at the speed you don't want, they suck you in, they cave you in, your energy and harms your organs.

S - The whirl (a sensation I felt when I received this weapon as it was being fired) is me and the machine and I have a piece of equipment for it and it ain't fucking invisible. And you could find it if you wanted, it's a joint effort, the missile gets fired and I encircle it around your energy - I direct it as it heads through the ozone layer, I have to help it on its way with me old weapon which is physical, the ozone layer gets in our fucking way, we ain't doing nothing to help it that's for sure, we'd like it a bit thinner Steve attends a meeting twice a year in the Royal Albert Hall, England and kills, using weapon Number 1, those standing in their way. He describes how he killed a scientist in England this October. These deaths occur simultaneously and the usual reason given is a heart attack. Surely this should be investigated

S - One of the ways we do it is we get together in one of our big groups and then we zap people and you could be on that list, people in our vicinity. We meet in Royal Albert Hall, we wouldn't mind meeting in a dome (the millennium dome) in London. We take it over for a night, all night, no one else is there and that's including the people that work there unless they are one of us and some of them are. We arrive about 1:00am and leave at 4:00am. We do this a few times a year, a society meeting. I am a freemason when I go to these meetings -- we are freemasons but we ain't. Fucking freemasons we just call ourselves that for the purpose of coming up with some excuse for why we want to turn up like we do. We are the freemasons, they aren't all us but a lot of them are. It's a certain part of the freemasons that meet up; the other freemasons ain't got a clue. I've just had one in the UK in October, its twice a year, we kill a few people that are well known, politicians and the like. We kill a few scientists now and again. There was one scientist we killed in October, quite a well-known scientist. I tell you that now we've been known to kill a few journalists if they snoop around. We killed this scientist in October, he's been in the papers, he was a young geezer - it wasn't no heart, sometimes we use CVA's to kill people, (I think it was a mysterious death) he was into research, he was a bit into physics - he was working on something we didn't want him to work on - yes I helped kill him.

Weapon Number 2

This weapon is an everyday weapon the Suppressive force use. I experienced it as though out of the blue I was swamped by what felt like a thick cloud. I was tense disorientated. Evidence that energy was used is that water (a lengthy power shower) removed it.

S - The bullets are me (toxic energy fired at a person). I have a little piece of equipment in my pocket so to speak which I carry around with me and use whenever I fucking want to - that ain't just at 3:00am - I can use it during the day too - as you found out. Then I visualize the person and then send it to their location and I just fire it off - we make it- the UK makes some of them and other places make them too.

Q - What size?

S - Its little - hand held - a bit bigger than a pat of butter - not a lot - its circular - its solid but its slim - I keep it in my wallet sometimes - I do it when I'm driving I just press a button and there it goes- when I'm queuing in traffic whenever I want. Yeah its flat alright - thicker than a credit card - if anyone found it they wouldn't have a clue what it is - its hard as nails there is no way you could have snapped it in two

Weapon Number 3

This weapon I received for eight months. Steve put in an implant and I received what he terms as toxic energy from midday until 10:00pm. They use this on antigovernment writers to reduce their work output. The effects are tension, inability to focus, and heaviness. Water removes this weapon, a long (at least 20 minutes preferably an hour) Jacuzzi/hot tub (the jets speed up the removal) is preferable. This again is evidence that toxic energy is involved.

S - It makes people feel heavy, depressed, not clear thinking, can't function as well, the afternoon blues, that's what it does. So we can control you better, to suppress you. So if you are under the weather you ain't geared up for anything and we get the better of you.

S - Its toxic energy - our machine manufactures it and shoots it at the person - as long as they are within our zone - way out to sea they'll be OK

S - Hours - 10.30am-ish until 9.00pm right now (winter) and 11.30am-ish until 10.00pm in the summer.

Q - Who receives this weapon?

S - Fucking common, we use this big time so you can bet you bottom teeth that anyone we don't want has got one.

S - Prince Charles, Dalai Llama, Tony Blair - most politicians receive it unless they are us. The queen.

Q - Why?

S - Because we want her to snuff it. This weapon brings you bad health, you snuff it earlier. If we want someone to die a bit earlier than they should then we put it on don't we. Princess Margaret got it. We want them all dead so we can take over.

President Bush gets it so we can control him better. Any powerful bloke gets it; all the politicians have it.

S - It's our machines that give you these weapons. The timer it's all done by a machine - our machine is fucking incredible.

DNA Samples

My own DNA sample was taken unknown to me. My intellect was assessed and my cancer risk found to be moderately high.

S - I've collected at least a 1000 samples.

S - I take brain sample.

Q - What with?

S - A piece of equipment.

Q - When?

S - When you are fucking snoring and I see to it that you are snoring.

Q - How?

S - The women have to fucking stay the night - the sex bit is up to me.

S - I knock them out, about 3:00am is the usual time.

Q - Where do you access the brain?

S – In between your soft tissue and your skull. I don't need to go through the skull; there will be a slight hole. Sometimes I choose the nostril or the hairline so you don't notice. I get a miniature sample and I give it to one of my mates, we meet and he takes it - in the UK - in the London area.

Education

S - Education one of the main things we are into behind the scenes.

S - We make the rules, we dish it out, we're on the board of directors in top universities, and we write the national curriculum. We bog you down with it as much as we can get away with.

Q - Why?

S - To control your minds, we don't want you thinking about other things. We don't fucking like any English - we'd rather you didn't do it - so you can't read and write - can't put pen to paper. We can't have you thinking for yourself and complaining. If people thought for themselves, the Republican's in the U.S. would never get elected. We control the neoconservatives as well.

Q - How should education really be?

S - They used to teach kids in medieval times to read and write and that's all you need, the rest you can learn other ways. Numbers - a bit of math, maybe a language or two, the rest they can learn if they are interested e.g. geography - you learn what you want to learn and not what's forced on you. Send your kids to an alternative school, or keeps them at home and teach them yourself. If it shows interest in academic things, then look at sending it somewhere where it can get normal qualifications so it can get the job it wants.

Crop Circles, Aliens and UFOs

Q - Crop circles they're caused by spaceships aren't they - the Greys?

S - We use it a bit we fabricate them so none of you believe - we put fakes in and then expose it to put you off the sent, but some of them are real - the old ones are real. But the new ones ain't, well some are but not many.

S - The small aliens (the Greys), we're not at war with them or anything, and it's none of their fucking business. We slaughter them if we can. They are pretty quick on the draw, nippy bastards and they can defend themselves - they want us to leave.

Q - How are the Greys involved with the force field? (He had previously mentioned how the Greys are trying to prevent them erecting a forcefield).

S - The Greys are trying to prevent us doing it aren't they.

Q - How?

S - They're negotiating with us, they want us to hold off and they'll leave us be. They are there for you and wish you fucking realized it, slagging them off Christ all mighty. They're getting slapped in the face for doing their bit for you.

Q - So what's going to happen?

S - So I suppose we're going to restart it because right now we're doing nothing because we've agreed kind of thing, but then we're going to restart when they fucking sod off because that's what they said they'd do.

Q - How long on hold for?

S - It's been a while - we would have completed it by now if it weren't for them.

Q - Why 20 years? (He had mentioned a forcefield being erected within 20 years).

Q - So you're developing these force field machines?

S - Yes that's it - in America - it's top secret, one of those places - so the greys haven't got a clue.

Q - Is it NASA?

S - Yes it is in NASA - the space places, we're developing them right under their noses.

Q - What do you say to the people working on them?

S - We tell our workers that they are space equipment.

Q - What do you tell them about the force field?

S - They think it is some way of holding other beings in place.

Q - What beings?

S - Well we tell them it's for the reptilians but obviously it ain't, they know there are reptilians, the NASA people.

Q - How?

S - Because they were attacked by them - some of their spacecrafts have run into reptilian places and been zapped because we don't want them nosing around.

Q - What NASA bases?

S - We've got it going in a few places in America - sometimes its NASA sometimes it's not. There is one in New Mexico; I think it's called Dulce.

SUPPRESSED TESLA AND OTHER INCREDIBLE TECHNOLOGIES

Ten Things You Should Know About Scalar Weapons
By Christi Verismo

Brace Yourself for a Scalar Weapon War That Could Occur Anytime!

1. A POSSIBLE SCALAR WAR SCENARIO

This seems like SF, but scalar beam weapons were invented in 1904 by Nikola Tesla (1856 or 57 – 1943) who was born in Yugoslavia. Many nations have secretly developed scalar technology, which now have myriad applications e.g. make a nuclear like destruction; earthquake; hurricane; tidal wave; cause instant freezing; cause intense heat like a burning fireball over a wide area; induce hypnotic mind control over a whole population; read any person on the planet's mind by remote; affect anybody's REM dream sleep by sending in subliminal pictures to the visual cortex; cause hallucinogen drug like effects or the symptoms of chemical or biological poisoning; make a disease epidemic by imprinting the disease 'signature' right into the cellular structure; paralyze and or/kill everyone instantaneously in a 50 mile radius and lastly remove something right out of its place in time and space faster than the speed of light, without any detectable warning with any target able to be fired at even right through the earth to it's antipodes.

If a scalar weapon armed country e.g. U.S. or Russia were to fire a nuclear missile to attack each other, this may not even reach the target, because the missile could be destroyed with scalar technology before it even left its place or origin. The knowledge via radio waves that it was about to be fired could be eavesdropped and the target could be destroyed in the bunker, fired at from space by armed satellite.

Alternatively invisible moving barriers and globes made of plasma (produced by crossed scalar beams) could destroy any nuclear missile easily while it moves along and detonate or dud it. Failing this, it could be destroyed by entering the target's territory containing a Tesla shield that would destroy anything entering its airspace.

To begin with, defense using scalar technology could destroy it before it even left the silo. Secret eavesdropping of radio communications tapping into ordinary military radio contact using undetectable 'scalar wave carriers' hacking in may have heard military personnel say it was about to be fired.

The missile could also be destroyed from above the site, by a cloaked UFO (American or Russian made anti-gravity disk originally made by back engineering crashed alien saucers) or cloaked aircraft using scalar or particle beams could undetectably (with standard equipment) cause the target to malfunction.

By using a scalar wave (radar like) 'interference grid', which covers both country's entire military activities in the air, underground or undersea, scalar transmitters transmit waves over large areas at 90 deg angles to each other. These waves follow the earth-ionospheric wave-guide and curve around the planet. The 'interference grid' shows solid moving objects as a spot of light moving through marked grid squares on an operator's video screen.

Scalar waves are a higher frequency than radar waves, and pass through solid things. As a focused beam they can target anything through the earth or sea. Crossed beams can produce explosions. This interference grid method could enable scalar beams to explode the missile before or after launch, as well as en route with knowing the right coordinates, by sending an earth curving beam one way then another combining at the target.

If the target does manage to launch, what are known as Tesla globes or Tesla hemispheric shields can be sent to envelop a missile or aircraft. These are made of luminous plasma which manifests physically from crossed scalar beams and can be created any size, even over 100 miles across. Initially detected and tracked as it moves on the scalar interference grid, a continuous EMP (electromagnetic pulse) Tesla plasma globe could kill the electronics of the target.

More intensely hot Tesla 'fireball' globes could vaporize the missile. Tesla globes could also activate a missile's nuclear warhead en route by creating a violent low order nuclear explosion. Various parts of the flying debris can be subjected to smaller more intense Tesla globes where the energy density to destroy is more powerful than the larger globe first encountered. This can be done in pulse mode with any remaining debris given maximum continuous heating to vaporize metals and materials. If anything still rains down on Russia or America, either could have already made a Tesla shield over the targeted area to block it from entering their airspace.

2. HOW WERE SCALAR WAVES DISCOVERED?

Scalar wave-forms are finer than gamma rays or X rays and only one hundred millionth of a square centimeter in width. They belong to the subtle gravitational field and are also known as gravitic waves. Uniquely, they flow in multiple directions at right angles off electromagnetic waves, as an untapped energy source called 'potentials'. Potentials are particles that are unorganized in hyperspace - pure etheric energy not coming through to the physical world.

Scalar waves were originally detected by a Scot, James Clerk Maxwell (1831-1879). He linked electricity and magnetism and laid the foundation for modern physics, but unfortunately Maxwell's 'potentials' were deliberately left out of his foundation work, which was taught in physics as a discipline, at colleges. Potentials were judged too "mystical" and only existed in the "ethers".

Nikola Tesla accidentally rediscovered them. He'd originally worked with Thomas Edison who discovered direct current, but Tesla discovered alternating current. Tesla found, while experimenting with violently abrupt direct current electrical charges, that a new form of energy (scalar) came through. By 1904, Tesla was able to harness scalar energy from one transmitter to another, undetectably bypassing time and space. It was just sucked right out of the hyperspace, into a transmitter and then into a beam that could be targeted to another transmitter. Scalar energy is still not acknowledged in mainstream physics because there is no money to be made from it travelling through wires.

3. A CLOSER LOOK AT SCALAR WAVE-FORMS

These finer scalar wave-forms also have been discovered periodically by other mathematicians, who have been able to calculate new equations especially in harmonics (used in hyperdimensional physics) connecting the wavelengths of matter, gravity and light to each other and how all these lock in and create our expression of time (as it manifests in space) - which has now been discovered to be untapped 'potential' energy flowing in hyperspace.

Time flows like a wave-form river in hyperspace in a grid pattern. This consists of interlocking great circles that circle the poles and include a lattice grid of lines that are 30 nautical miles or 55.5 km apart. When scalar beams charge through hyperspace these 'rivers of time' get blocked and redirected temporarily.

There is a covert plan underfoot to change the way time is expressed on this planet altogether using hyperdimensional physics and Tesla technology, by splicing earth back onto a now defunct Atlantean timeline in which Lucifer hadn't fallen from grace, (see my other work on this in the books *The Universal Seduction* Vols 2 and 3 at the end of this article).

Our present 'reality' is expressed in the way time runs around the corridors in hyperspace by the pattern it takes. Other 'timelines' exist in a different kind of grid pattern, creating alternative versions of our 'present'. Multiple versions of 'reality' (or for example 2 April 2004) can be manipulated given the right technology, and people can enter into parallel universes do all sorts of things and then return back into this one. One needs a Tesla Zero Time Reference Generator, which can lodge a specific reality into the time at the center of the universe, (in which time stays still), acting like an anchor. Both America and the UK governments are able to manipulate and enter into different realities.

The various dimensions each comprise a complex pattern of interlocking wave-forms. Matter has been found to be only one wave of a pulse comprising a positive cycle, while the negative cycle manifests as 'anti-matter'. The 'matter' pulse brings something 'into' physical visibility, it disappears momentarily and returns. But the pulses are so rapid we don't see something as unmanifest while temporarily dematerializing. Physical time is only measured by the visibility of something's aging process, or in other words its passage through a journey starting at one measured time-reference point to another.

Different wave-forms only appear to us to be solid because we are comprised of the same matter. If the frequencies governing the time between a matter pulse and an anti-matter pulse are shortened or lengthened with technology, time will go faster or slower in the surrounding space or where it effects. Therefore, scalar waves belong to space-time in which anti-matter or hyperspace exists.

Time can be altered by harnessed and directed scalar waves (including magnets which give off scalar waves and which can bend time) because they disrupt the pulse of matter and anti-matter and therefore the rate at which something normally passes through time with its usual smoothness. An experiment with scalar waves in USA once caused all the clocks and watches in the test neighborhood to go berserk for four days, until the flow of time resettled back to its normal flow and they returned as before.

Scalar 'potentials' can be created artificially and when focused into a weapon, can do major damage to an object's location in space-time. That which determines the object's natural pulse of matter and anti-matter cycle can become stressed when targeted by scalar waves, because they are almost always absorbed by the nucleus of an atom, not the electrons in orbit.

Hyperspace can become warped temporarily, although space-time naturally curves around natural vortexes the earth has, which form chakras to absorb and release universal energies. These are opened and closed in natural cycles according to the positions of the sun and moon in relation to earth.

Scalar waves pass through any physical substance undetected, however, when focused into a beam the damage inflicted can be so powerful that they can dislodge an object right out of time and space and cause it to temporarily disappear away from its normal movement in time. All objects move in time, and they will also move in space if a physical external force activates the object's own natural internal scalar waves to focus in the direction it which it is sent, causing it to move from A to B.

An object is trapped motionless in space by the internal scalar energy within swirling around interlocking into a deadlock, (making it appear still) however the object still moves in time. A beam of scalar energy can cause the timeframe the object moves along in to get warped, making it disappear into another reality.

4. HOW DO SCALAR WEAPONS WORK?

Artificially made 'potentials' can be harnessed into multiple frequency scalar waves. If a transmitter is at a higher reference potential than the 'interference zone' of 2 crossed scalar beams, energy emerges into the plasma 'bottle' which will materialize physically and this is called 'exothermic' mode. This can cause explosions and can be 'nuclear like' if set at a high frequency. Even though no electromagnetic energy has flown through space between the transmitters and the target, and because it has bypassed physical space, the energy can suddenly appear faster than the speed of light and destroy something without warning.

It is only locked in artificial potential that is a directed 'river of force' in hyperspace and it is entirely undetectable with conventional scientific equipment, which is where the danger lies. Nobody can ever know what the enemy is planning or who their enemies are and because it never gets any press normal military personnel without this knowledge would never know what hit them, especially if it is scalar mind control. All technical equipment can be dudded inexplicably too.

To extract energy back to the transmitters from the energy bottle of two crossed scalar beams, the potential must be set at a lower mode and this is called 'endothermic' mode and as energy is extracted out of the 'bottle' area, a freezing will occur, possibly causing a thunderous sound. When two transmitters send timed pulses, which meet, an explosion will occur which either produces energy or extracts it.

If two crossed beams are in 'continuous' mode the energy between beams is continuous and Tesla globes and hemispheres can be made which act as a continuous shield to either destroy incoming weapons and aircraft entering it. If multiple frequencies are transmitted on the beams, at the intersection a three-dimensional globe appears. This can be manipulated to have very high infolded energy with any desired light emission, shape, color, size or intensity. It can even cause metal to soften or melt. This 'bottle' of energy can be detonated inside the earth to create an earthquake, erupt a volcano or into a building to make a 'nuclear like' explosion and can be moved anywhere on the planet or through it.

The Russians in 1985 once threatened the earth itself by activating their scalar weapons with multiple scalar transmitters turned on at once, endangering the survival of the entire planet. According to nuclear physicist Tom Bearden, they conducted a massive, 'full up' scalar weapon systems and communications strategic exercise. During this sudden exercise Frank Golden discovered and monitored the Russians activating 27 gigantic 'power taps', established by resonating the earth electrogravitationally on 54 powerful scalar frequencies (27 pairs where the two are separated from each other by 12 kHz.) transmitted into the earth and they utilized this to stimulate the earth into forced electrogravitational resonance on all 54 frequencies. Each of the 27 power taps extracted enormous energy from the molten core of the earth itself, and turning it into ordinary electrical power. Each giant tap is capable of powering 4 to 6 of the largest scalar EM howitzers possessed by Russia.

Bearden writes: "Apparently over 100 giant scalar EM weapons were activated and a large number of command and control transmissions and it lasted several days. By alternating the potentials and loads of each of the two paired transmitters, electrical energy in enormous amounts can be extracted from the earth itself, fed by the 'giant cathode' that is the earth's molten core. Scalar EM command and control systems, including high data rate communications with underwater submarines, were also activated on a massive scale. The exercise went on for several days, as power taps were switched in and out, and command and control systems went up and down." Bearden also monitored it and claimed that not one US lab or scientist detected this and to this day, not one officially believes it ever happened.

The Soviets are using unknown attributes of matter, phenomena and laws of nature by research covering the equivalent of 7-8 U.S. atom bomb projects back to back already. However both America and Russia are doing through the earth scalar beam transmissions and ever since then earth's internal dynamo has been affected. It suddenly experienced a sudden unexpected slowdown in rotation 1984. It has become like an unbalanced washing machine, wobbling as it spins. Natural solar scalar waves pass naturally between the center of the earth and the sun, and this coupled with multiple annual nuclear tests, (which have been proven to disturb the ionosphere and magnetic field) the balance of the earth with the moon, may even cause the earth to flip, if solar produced scalar waves are diverted onto another course, which should be keeping the earth spinning harmoniously.

5. WHAT CAN SCALAR WEAPONS DO?

If two timed scalar pulses meet, an explosion extraction can make a sharp cooling and all heated energy is extracted out of the air back to the transmitter. This can make everything and everyone frozen. It preserves machines and buildings but not people. If a burning energy is sent the target has a nuclear like 'detonation' because energy emerges to a target destroying the nucleus of the atoms. Multiple scalar wave modes and frequencies can also be blended together into one beam as well.

A Tesla shield, shaped like a dome protecting a military target could be made of three or more concentric shields that would produce multiple electromagnetic pulse energy and severe heating of anything that enters it. Concentric Tesla shields can also clean up and sterilize any gamma radiation resulting from an explosion of a nuclear warhead. Tesla even in the 1920s could create these.

This acted like an electrifying force field, which could cause anything which entered it to have its technology dudded, make incoming aircraft pilots die by destroying their nervous system and/or make an incoming missile, aircraft or tank blow up. Multiple layers could be nested made of different kinds of plasmas that would ensure nothing could penetrate a protected target's groundspace or airspace.

Commander X's Guide to Incredible Conspiracies

The Russians can make a Tesla shield up to 200 miles wide and shields and globes have been occasionally seen over the oceans. Scalar beams can travel right through the earth and create an earthquake at the antipodes of the earth. Tesla also experimented doing this. Many intense frequency small globes can be directed towards multiple incoming targets, like cannonballs causing major explosions. Alternatively a larger less intense globe sent can cause the electrics to dud in a plane, helicopter or missile causing it to malfunction and crash land. This technology has been used many times to crash planes or helicopters by using a portable scalar bazooka carried by a hidden terrorist or soldier.

Scalar waves can be used for impenetrable communication inside an ordinary carrier wave. Artificial potentials can be used for two-way communication with submarines, aircraft and ships. Scalar waves can be used to tap into normal communications even when encrypted. They can even destroy the enemy's equipment if they wish using 'lock-in' mode to locate the source or just continue eavesdropping.

Radar invisibility can be done by putting multiple transmitters around something to make a spherical interference shell in the bandwidth of the searching radar. Nothing in the air is safe with scalar weapons or anything on the ground, because any building can be penetrated and the inside contents destroyed. There is nowhere to hide. Scalar beams can be sent by aircraft or satellite or even from the government UFOs of Russia, Britain, Australia and America. They can be sent from the UFOs the Nazis developed secretly in Germany during WW2, and which were relocated to their underground bases in Antarctica and all over South America before the war ended.

6. SCALAR BEAMS AGAINST INDIVIDUALS

To totally destroy a person's nervous system and kill them instantaneously, a scalar weapon can be set on 'high intensity pulse mode'. This will destroy every living cell, bacteria and all germs so the body falls down like a limp rag, not even decaying in even 30-45 days. There is no living aspect left to decay. Entire groups of people can be killed this way even in a 50-mile radius on peak power. Scalar beams set on a lower power can render a person unconscious to be revived at a later date for interrogation.

Crossed scalar beams can cover a whole range of targets from something right through the other side of the earth, to anything under the sea or ground. Not even metal will suffice to protect, as a metal softening mode can be deployed. Scalar beams can be put into 'X ray' mode where a screen can show what is inside something, even under the sea and earth or inside buildings.

This is called a remote viewing radar. Anything in the sky can be instantly destroyed even from one country to another with the interference grid to cause anything even under the earth and sea that enters it to be destroyed. The explosion shows up on the video screen as a blossoming of the moving light on the square, the operator knows a target has been hit.

Tom Bearden claims since the 1960s the Russians mainly use their interference grids over the USA to control the weather moving hot or cold air where they can meet and create storms, hurricanes, torrential rain or droughts as they please. Earthquakes can be created with the grid along with volcanoes erupting. Moisture can be brought from the ocean and sent overland and cold air from the north sent south. Violent thunderstorms can be created.

Commander X's Guide to Incredible Conspiracies

In 1989 the Japanese Yazuka and Aum sects leased scalar interferometers from the Russians to do weather engineering over the USA. However America can fight back with scalar weapons of their own. One can silently down passenger planes as need be by sending low frequency scalar beam to make the engine fail, either pinpointing a target with the interference grid squares or using portable shoulder scalar weapon bazookas, which can be fired at any aircraft above. Surface naval vessels can be attacked through their hulls as well as ocean bottom mines detonated. Any aircraft, or land vessels including tanks can be fitted with scalar weapons and destroyed with them.

7. SCALAR MIND CONTROL

In the early 1970's hundreds of Utah State Prison inmates were subjected to scalar wave mind control, unsuccessfully fighting back in court. The University of Utah researched how scalar waves could induce the mind into hearing voices, overriding and implanting thoughts into the mind, as well as reading the thoughts. They also developed eye implants. In 1998 scalar waves were used to test subliminal voices in the head, in two Utah prisons.

In Draper Prison, Utah an inmate, David Fratus in 1988, claimed voices in his inner ears were induced in him as clear as if listening to a set of stereo headphones. The mind control victims of US govt. implants are also subjected to artificial voices in the head which are sent on scalar beam by satellite and the HAARP transmitters and relayed to the GWEN Towers placed approx. every 200 miles across USA. Many of the messages relayed into these American mind control victims are said to come from aliens, with a 'message for mankind'. These 'alien messages' were first given to the prisoners in Utah and they all got the same messages.

The U.S. can now whip up the masses into a genocidal frenzy and according to Joe Vialls, in 1994 the Hutus and Tutsis in Rwanda were mind controlled by C-130 Hercules aircraft containing mind control technology and the rage coming on suddenly over groups of people was repeated hundreds of times by the C-130 Hercules passing over. With transmitters using precise accuracy to three decimal places brain waves can be controlled to induce rage, fear, panic, lethargy and vomiting etc. They first made sure the Hutus were armed to start off the Rwandan war. The Hutus had glazed eyes and went from anger to uncontrollable rage in minutes after the direct pass of the American aircraft.

All that needs to be known is the width of the crowd to adjust the microwave aerials to focus the beam over the crowd. American agents in Kigali initially ramped up public suspicion about foul play in the presidential air crash. The whole Rwandan American terminal mind control experiment was called "Operation Crimson Mist" and has been repeated on a smaller scale in Iraq. Vialls claims this ability has been known since the 1950s.

The Russians, having a head start on decoding the brain can send subliminal messages by satellite over whole countries in their own languages, in scalar waves so subtle that the victims think they are their own thoughts occurring. They could make people think "God" is speaking to them and can also give a people suicidal thoughts. There is a suicide wavelength.

Americans have been using these subliminals to give 'voices in the head' messages (which includes to those with CIA or military controlled implants) from

106

"aliens" and now "The Holy Spirit" to say e.g. the Second Coming will be here soon or earth needs to be evacuated and the person has been 'chosen'.

Only certain people can pick this up according to whether they have implants (which relay messages into the head) or if they are natural telepathics. The mineral selenium when ingested beyond normal levels is said to increase the capacity to hear voices in the head. Though certain races have a higher hearing threshold and are able to pick up synthetic telepathy sent through the atmosphere more than others.

Russia's scalar transmitters are called "Woodpeckers" because of the woodpecker type tapping transmissions detected from them on the radio band. They have the technology to send subliminals right into a person's subconscious, bypassing the brain and could drastically influence the thoughts, vision, physical functioning, emotions and conscious state of a person by sending in subliminal signals even from a great distance. In the late 1960s the Soviets broke the genetic code of the human brain. It had 44 digits or less and employed 22 frequency bands across nearly the whole EM spectrum. But only 11 of the frequency bands were independent.

The Soviets found they could make a person do something just by sending subliminals into the body, bypassing the ears. Up to 16 of the Russian Woodpecker scalar transmitters have been observed to carry a common phase-locked 10 Hz modulation. 10 Hz is used to put people into a hypnotic state. The Russians can manipulate the moods of everyone in a 75-mile radius, with a circularly polarized antenna, and people's bodies have been shown to pick up the "new" mode of expression. Even "sleep" frequency will make everyone tired and fall asleep. In the UK transmitters are placed all over to regulate the moods of the population according to Tim Rifat.

8. AMERICA'S 'NO CONTACT' MASS MIND CONTROLLING NETWORK

In *Project L.U.C.I.D* by Texe Marrs, John St Clair Akwei claims that the NSA has had the most advanced computers in the world since the 1960's. NSA uses scalar waves for blanket coverage of the USA and can wirelessly tap into any computer in the USA and read the contents. As well as track people by the electrical currents in their bodies, which emanates a particular 'signature frequency'.

Everything in the environment gives off scalar waves at right angle rotations off the normal electromagnetic wave. These can be searched for and tracked and are not subject to constraints of time and space. A person's frequency can be stored on a supercomputer and this can be tracked anywhere. Their voice can also be located among millions of phone calls by its signature.

One can be sent subliminal words sent in scalar waves that are so subtle that the person will think they are their own thoughts. Also NSA uses a secret program (developed since the MKULTRA mind control program of the 1950s) what is called "Radiation Intelligence". Scientific research from this is withheld from the public and there are international intelligence agreements to keep this technology secret. Using this technology the NSA records and decodes individual brain maps of hundreds of thousands of people for national security purposes. It is also used secretly by the military for a brain-to-computer link. Activity in the speech center of the brain can be translated into the subject's verbal thoughts and can also show up activity from their visual cortex on a video monitor.

NSA operatives can see what the subject is seeing. Visual memory can also be seen and the NSA can place images directly into the visual cortex, bypassing the eyes and the optic nerves. When a target sleeps secretly images can be installed into the brain during REM sleep for brain-programming purposes. Speech, 3D sound, and subliminal audio can also be sent to the auditory cortex of the brain, bypassing the ears.

This "Remote Neural Monitoring" (RNM) can completely alter a subject's perception, moods and motor control. Different brainwave frequencies are connected with various parts of the body and when the right frequency to activate a section of the body is sent a person is powerless to stop it. Pain can be induced in mind control victims this way by targeting a section of the body. This has been spoken of by many mind control victims, accompanied by 'voices in the head' spoken by the operators cruelly asking if it hurt and all done remotely without any physical contact with the victim. Though some say they have implants.

There has been a NSA 'SIGINT' wireless scalar wave brain monitoring network in the U.S. since the 1940s according to John St Clair Akwei. He tells us how it is done with digitally decoding the evoked 'potentials' in the 30-50Hz, five-milliwatt electromagnetic emissions from the brain. In these emissions spikes and patterns show as evoked potentials.

Every thought, reaction, motor command, auditory event and visual image in the brain has a corresponding 'evoked potential' or set of 'evoked potentials'. These can be decoded into the current thoughts, images and sounds going on in a target's brain. When complexly coded signals are sent to a victim, bypassing the eyes, optic nerves and ears, the faint images appear as floating 2D screens in the brain. Auditory hallucinations can be induced, creating paranoid schizophrenia.

9. IS THERE A SECRET WAR GOING IN THE SKIES?

Japan now has scalar weapons and has got together with Russia to develop them. In 1989 The Russians leased the Japanese the super-secret intercontinental scalar weapons, capable of producing earthquakes for $900 million, which they'd used in the Soviet Union since the 1960's. A Joint Russian-Japanese university was set up to develop new weapons with Japanese microchips to overpower the US and jointly rule the world.

After Tesla died in 1943, his papers were sent to a Tesla Museum in Yugoslavia, where the Japanese obtained the knowledge of Tesla technology. The scalar weapons were developed by a Japanese scientist with an IQ higher than Einstein.

They too, like the Americans tested their scalar weapons in the outback of Western Australia, possibly using a base in Antarctica in which to send scalar waves to their Australian transmitter to produce earthquakes and Tesla globes. It is the Japanese Aum sect and Yakuza mafia who are still leasing the Russian scalar transmitters to target the U.S., they have a policy of exacting revenge and they are connected with the North Korean cults.

10. WHO ELSE IS CONTINUING TESLA'S SCALAR TECHNOLOGY?

Eastern Europe and Russia include Tesla's scalar wave research in their curriculum and made multiple scalar weapon transmitters over the Soviet Union starting from the 1950's. America, found out they'd been secretly attacked during the 1950's undetected by the Soviets. In 1960 the Soviet premier Kruschev announced to the world, that they had "superweapons".

Commander X's Guide to Incredible Conspiracies

In 1963 they deliberately destroyed a U.S. atomic submarine undersea by Puerto Rico with scalar weapons. They next day over the Puerto Rico Trench the Soviets used scalar weapons in a different mode to produce a giant underwater explosion. The U.S. was defenseless against an unknown type of weapon. In 1965 the Great Sandy Desert in W Australia was chosen by the U.S. govt. to begin scalar weapons testing from Tesla's knowledge. The U.S. military tested crossed scalar beams aimed into the desert ground to create earthquakes on a target map of squares and also created Tesla globes from crossed scalar beams in the sky.

Pine Gap the secret underground American military base has two scalar transmitters and they also have at least another in Exmouth, N Western Australia. Others American scalar transmitters besides various ones in USA, including Maine are at Alaska, Puerto Rico, Greenland, Norway and Antarctica.

Though many countries have scalar weapons now, other countries could easily be target of those with scalar weapons and never know what the cause of their explosions, mind control or weather engineering. So of course more and more countries are getting the scalar technology needing it to defend themselves as well and this keeps getting passed on especially by the Russians.

The other thing is one may know it is a scalar attack but have no idea who did it. The known countries which have scalar weapons are: America, Russia, France, Australia, Germany, Japan, China, Taiwan, South Africa, Israel, Brazil, UK and Argentina as well as various populations of Nazis still operating in Antarctica and all over South America.

It is unknown how Brazilians got scalar weapons and quantum potential weapons, but the Brazilians have had alien technology for some time and also the Vatican has covert technology and has been said to have a base for this in South America for their secret space program. There is extensive coverage of Brazil's space program in my 40 page article "Scalar Weapons: Read it and Weep". This covers China and Japan's weapons as well as extensive coverage of Russia's attacks on America, especially the space shuttles and the technology of the Nazis in Antarctica.

Others may have them such as Ukraine and Nth Korea but as yet no proof exists for these countries. Even in the alternative press not enough has been said about scalar weapons to the extent where normal conspiracy researchers and writers are as familiar with their dangers as they should be. Even online, these "ultimate" weapons scarcely receive the attention they deserve.

For more information see the book: *The Universal Seduction* Vol. 3: Scalar Weapons. *Read It And Weep* by Christi Verismo - http://www.theuniversalseduction.com

Christi Verismo website for an extended version of this article plus more articles:
http://www.angelfire.com/oz/cv

Nikola Tesla and the Search for Free Energy
By Tim Swartz, Editor of Conspiracy Journal - www.conspiracyjournal.com

Our civilization depends on energy to survive. Throughout the centuries we have come up with a myriad of different methods to extract energy for our needs. Our first energy resources were our very own muscles. If something had to be moved, say a big rock, a large group of people got together to push and pull until the rock was where it was supposed to be. Of course this type of energy was limited by the overall strength that human muscles could provide; so beasts of burden were domesticated and a whole new source of energy was made available to our infant society.

It wasn't long, however, before oxen and horses were no longer enough to carry mankind into an industrial society. Eventually someone noticed that burning things, all kinds of things, provided energy that could be used in all sorts of interesting applications.

Burning things could produce heat for warmth and cooking; and best of all, burning things could change water into steam to turn engines and turbines. Thus, began the great era of burning as mankind now sought the perfect fuel for their energy wants and needs.

Considering how far mankind has come since then, it is amazing that with all of our science and technology we still haven't gotten beyond burning things for energy. We may have become more efficient at it; oil is more energetic than wood – nuclear fusion is more efficient than oil – but we are still burning nevertheless.

We now know that burning things is not a very good idea, both for our overall health and the health of the environment. But presently, there doesn't seem to be any better solution to our growing energy needs. Or is there?

The big energy companies say that "alternative" energies such as solar, wind, and thermal, just will not generate the power necessary to run all of our technological stuff. Only oil, they say, and maybe nuclear, has the energy potential to keep our cars running and our air conditioners cooling. However, there are annoying mavericks that claim there are other sources of energy that are cheap, abundant and clean.

The great scientist and creator of our modern electrical system, Nikola Tesla, was just one of those men that the big oil companies hated having around. Even though Tesla lived in the early 20th century, he had 21st century ideas and visions.

Tesla believed in all-pervading aether. He felt the aether was always in motion, that this motion was the basis of electricity, and ascribed all electric and magnetic phenomena to electrostatic molecular forces. With the advent of Einstein's Theory of Relativity, there was no longer room for the universal aether. However, modern Quantum and Superstring physics has resurrected the universal aether and given it a modern twist in the form of Zero Point Energy.

In 1891, Nikola Tesla in an address to the American Institute of Electrical Engineers, stated his belief that: "Soon, our machinery will be driven by a power obtainable at any point in the universe. This idea is not novel...We find it in the delightful myth of Antheus, who derives power from the earth; we find it among the subtle speculations of one of your splendid mathematicians...Throughout space there is energy. Is this energy static or kinetic? If static our hopes are in vain; if kinetic – and this we know it is, for certain – then it is a mere question of time when men will succeed in attaching their machinery to the very wheelwork of nature".

Commander X's Guide to Incredible Conspiracies

It appears that Tesla was thinking about Zero Point Energy years before other scientists had even tried to grasp the idea that the universe could be filled with almost unlimited energy.

"Electric power is everywhere," said Tesla. "Present in unlimited quantities and can drive the world's machinery without the need of coal, oil, gas, or any other of the common fuels".

What is Zero Point Energy?

Dutch physicist M J Sparnaay discovered the existence of Zero Point Electromagnetic Energy in 1958. Mr Sparnaay had continued the experiments carried out by Hendrik B G Casimir that showed the existence of a force between two uncharged parallel plates that arose from electromagnetic radiation surrounding the pates in a vacuum.

Mr Sparnaay discovered that the forces acting on the plates came not only from thermal energy, but also from electromagnetic Zero Point Energy. Mr Sparnaay determined that not only did the zero point electromagnetic energy exist in a vacuum, but also that it persisted even at a temperature of absolute zero.

This term Zero Point Energy comes from the concept that even if matter were cooled down to absolute zero in terms of its temperature, this energy still remains. It appears in theory that this energy is quite intense. Nobel Laureate Richard Feynman and one of Einstein's protégés, John Wheeler, calculated that there is more than enough energy in the volume of a coffee cup to evaporate all the worlds' oceans.

Special characteristics of Zero Point Energy are that it has a virtually infinite energy density and that it is ubiquitous (even present in outer space), and these make it very desirable as an energy source. Andre Sakharov, the Soviet Physicist, argued that we should regard all matter as floating in a sea of energy. Modern physics tells us that the universe is filled with vast amounts of fluctuating energy: fluctuations that are fundamental to our view of the fabric of nature.

The implication of this universal energy field is that since all physical matter can be considered to be floating in a sea of energy, it could be collected and converted into electrical energy, that could more than meet the world's ever growing demand for energy. Unfortunately, it seems that Zero Point Energy has so far eluded scientists, much to the joy of the already established energy companies who aren't eager for new competition.

The Tesla Electric Car

Aeronautical engineer, Derek Ahlers, while living in New York met with Peter Savo, a nephew of Nikola Tesla. Savo told Ahlers a number of interesting stories about Tesla's life and experiments, including one that took place in 1931.

Tesla asked Savo to accompany him on a long train ride to Buffalo, New York. Going into a small garage, Tesla showed his nephew a Pierce Arrow car. Oddly, under the hood, instead of the engine, there was an AC motor. This measured around three feet long, and a little more than two feet in diameter.

From it trailed two very thick cables that connected with the dashboard. In addition, there was an ordinary 12-volt storage battery. The motor was rated at 80 horsepower. Maximum rotor speed was stated to be 30 turns per second. A six-foot antenna was fitted into the rear section of the car.

Tesla stepped into the passenger side and began making adjustments on a "power receiver" which had been built directly into the dashboard. The receiver used 12 special tubes that Tesla had brought with him. Furthermore, two thick rods protruded from the converter housing. Tesla pushed them in saying: "Now we have power."

Tesla handed Savo the ignition key and told him to start the engine, which he promptly did. The motor was completely silent, yet when the accelerator was applied, the car instantly moved. Savo drove a distance of 50 miles through the city and out to the surrounding countryside. The car was tested to speeds of 90 mph and reportedly performed better than any internal combustion engine of its day.

Tesla informed his nephew that the device could not only supply the needs of the car forever, but could also supply the needs of a household – with power to spare. Of the motive source he referred to "a mysterious radiation that comes out of the aether and is available in limitless quantities".

The two remained in Buffalo for eight days, rigorously testing the car in the city and countryside. Tesla also told Savo that the device would soon be used to drive boats, planes, trains, and other automobiles.

A few months after this test and because of the economic crisis at the time, Pierce Arrow had to stop production. Savo asked his uncle whether or not the power receiver was being used in other applications other than the Pierce Arrow. He was informed that Tesla had been negotiating with a major shipbuilding company to build a boat with a similarly outfitted engine. However, Tesla refused to discuss his experiment further with his nephew.

Highly concerned and personally strained over the security of this design, it seems obvious that Tesla was performing these tests in a desperate degree of secrecy for good reasons. Tesla had in the past been the victim of theft of his patents and inventions and he had by this time become obsessed with secrecy. Unfortunately, Tesla's amazing car and the technology used to power it apparently died along with him. Or did it? Could it be that Tesla was the first to create a practical device to tap into Zero Point Energy?

Officially, the first Zero Point electromagnetic radiation energy patent was issued to Dr. Frank Mead on Dec. 31, 1996. Patent number 5,590,031 made history as Dr. Mead of Edwards Air Force Base designed spherical receivers to access zero point electromagnetic radiation. These receiving devices that convert neutrinos, gamma rays, tachyons to electricity require very high frequency receiver technology. Dr. Mead grapples with the high frequencies that may extend up to 10 to the 40th Hz (cycles per second). But so far Dr. Mead hasn't tried to replicate Nikola Tesla's retrofitted Pierce-Arrow experiment.

Zero Point Energy is by no means the only game in town when it comes to "Free Energy". Multiple methods for producing vast amounts of energy at extremely low cost have been developed. Even though there is good evidence that the military is using Zero Point Energy, none of these technologies has made it to the "open" consumer market. The reasons are numerous and complex, but greed and personal power play a large role in this suppression. Nevertheless, free energy technology is here. It is real, and someday it will change everything about the way we live and forever do away with the obsolete technology of burning things for energy.

Mind Control in the 21st Century
By Commander X

New methods of mind control technology were first introduced in the 1950s as an obscure branch of the CIA's MK-ULTRA project group. Just as organized crime is not stopped by hearings and court cases, neither did this originally obscure branch of MK-ULTRA activity, when the top secret operations were exposed by the U.S. Senate's Church-Inouye hearings in the late 1970s.

Since government-backed electronic mind control is classified at the highest levels in all technologically capable governments, the description of effects is taken from the personal experiences of over 300 known involuntary experimentees. The experimentees without exception report that once the "testing" begins, the classified experiment specification apparently requires that the "testing" be continued for life. Many test subjects are now in their 70s and 80s. Some have children and the children are often subjected to the same "testing" as their parent(s).

In an amazing article published by Spectra Magazine in 1999, author Rauni-Leena Luukanen-Kilde, MD, Former Chief Medical Officer of Finland, writes that in 1948 Norbert Weiner published a book, Cybernetics, defined as a neurological communication and control theory already in use in small circles at that time. Yoneji Masuda, "Father of the Information Society," stated his concern in 1980 that our liberty is threatened Orwellian-style by cybernetic technology totally unknown to most people. This technology links the brains of people via implanted microchips to satellites controlled by ground-based supercomputers.

The first brain implants were surgically inserted in 1974 in the state of Ohio and also in Stockholm, Sweden. Brain electrodes were inserted into the skulls of babies in 1946 without the knowledge of their parents. In the 1950s and 60s, electrical implants were inserted into the brains of animals and humans, especially in the U.S., during research into behavior modification, and brain and body functioning. Mind control (MC) methods were used in attempts to change human behavior and attitudes. Influencing brain functions became an important goal of military and intelligence services.

Thirty years ago brain implants showed up in X-rays the size of one centimeter. Subsequent implants shrunk to the size of a grain of rice. They were made of silicon, later still of gallium arsenide. Today they are small enough to be inserted into the neck or back, and intravenously in different parts of the body during surgical operations, with or without the consent of the subject. It is now almost impossible to detect or remove them.

It is technically possible for every newborn to be injected with a microchip, which could then function to identify the person for the rest of his or her life. Such plans are secretly being discussed in the U.S. without any public airing of the privacy issues involved. In Sweden, Prime Minister Olof Palme gave permission in 1973 to implant prisoners, and Data Inspection's ex-Director General Jan Freese revealed that nursing-home patients were implanted in the mid-1980s.

Implanted human beings can be followed anywhere. Their brain functions can be remotely monitored by supercomputers and even altered through the changing of frequencies. Guinea pigs in secret experiments have included prisoners, soldiers, mental patients, handicapped children, deaf and blind people, homosexuals, single women, the elderly, school children, and any group of people considered "marginal" by the elite experimenters. The published experiences of prisoners in Utah State Prison, for example, are shocking to the conscience.

Today's microchips operate by means of low-frequency radio waves that target them. With the help of satellites, the implanted person can be tracked anywhere on the globe. Such a technique was among a number tested in the Iraq war, according to Dr. Carl Sanders, who invented the intelligence-manned interface (IMI) biotic, which is injected into people. (Earlier during the Vietnam War, soldiers were injected with the Rambo chip, designed to increase adrenaline flow into the bloodstream.) The 20-billion-bit/second supercomputers at the U.S. National Security Agency (NSA) could now "see and hear" what soldiers experience in the battlefield with a remote monitoring system (RMS).

When a 5-micromillimeter microchip (the diameter of a strand of hair is 50 micromillimeters) is placed into optical nerve of the eye, it draws neuroimpulses from the brain that embody the experiences, smells, sights, and voice of the implanted person. Once transferred and stored in a computer, these neuroimpulses can be projected back to the person's brain via the microchip to be re-experienced. Using a RMS, a land-based computer operator can send electromagnetic messages (encoded as signals) to the nervous system, affecting the target's performance. With RMS, healthy persons can be induced to see hallucinations and to hear voices in their heads.

Every thought, reaction, hearing, and visual observation causes a certain neurological potential, spikes, and patterns in the brain and its electromagnetic fields, which can now be decoded into thoughts, pictures, and voices. Electromagnetic stimulation can therefore change a person's brain-waves and affect muscular activity, causing painful muscular cramps experienced as torture.

The NSA's electronic surveillance system can simultaneously follow and handle millions of people. Each of us has a unique bioelectrical resonance frequency in the brain, just as we have unique fingerprints. With electromagnetic frequency (EMF) brain stimulation fully coded, pulsating electromagnetic signals can be sent to the brain, causing the desired voice and visual effects to be experienced by the target. This is a form of electronic warfare. U.S. astronauts were implanted before they were sent into space so their thoughts could be followed and all their emotions could be registered 24 hours a day.

The *Washington Post* reported in May 1995 that Prince William of Great Britain was implanted at the age of 12. Thus, if he were ever kidnapped, a radio wave with a specific frequency could be targeted to his microchip. The chip's signal would be routed through a satellite to the computer screen of police headquarters, where the Prince's movements could be followed. He could actually be located anywhere on the globe.

The mass media has not reported that an implanted person's privacy vanishes for the rest of his or her life. S/he can be manipulated in many ways. Using different frequencies, the secret controller of this equipment can even change a person's emotional life. S/he can be made aggressive or lethargic. Sexuality can be artificially influenced. Thought signals and subconscious thinking can be read, dreams affected and even induced, all without the knowledge or consent of the implanted person.

A perfect cyber-soldier can thus be created. This secret technology has been used by military forces in certain NATO countries since the 1980s without civilian and academic populations having heard anything about it. Thus, little information about such invasive mind-control systems is available in professional and academic journals.

The NSA's Signals Intelligence group can remotely monitor information from human brains by decoding the evoked potentials (3.50HZ, 5 milliwatt) emitted by the brain. Prisoner experimentees in both Gothenburg, Sweden and Vienna, Austria have been found to have evident brain lesions. Diminished blood circulation and lack of oxygen in the right temporal frontal lobes result where brain implants are usually operative. A Finnish experimentee experienced brain atrophy and intermittent attacks of unconsciousness due to lack of oxygen.

Mind control techniques can be used for political purposes. The goal of mind controllers today is to induce the targeted persons or groups to act against his or her own convictions and best interests. Zombified individuals can even be programmed to murder and remember nothing of their crime afterward. Alarming examples of this phenomenon can be found in the U.S.

This "silent war" is being conducted against unknowing civilians and soldiers by military and intelligence agencies. Since 1980, electronic stimulation of the brain (ESB) has been secretly used to control people targeted without their knowledge or consent. All international human rights agreements forbid nonconsensual manipulation of human beings — even in prisons, not to speak of civilian populations.

Under an initiative of U.S. Senator John Glenn, discussions commenced in January 1997 about the dangers of radiating civilian populations. Targeting people's brain functions with electromagnetic fields and beams (from helicopters and airplanes, satellites, from parked vans, neighboring houses, telephone poles, electrical appliances, mobile phones, TV, radio, etc.) is part of the radiation problem that should be addressed in democratically elected government bodies.

In addition to electronic MC, chemical methods have also been developed. Mind-altering drugs and different smelling gasses affecting brain function negatively can be injected into air ducts or water pipes. Bacteria and viruses have also been tested this way in several countries.

Today's super-technology, connecting our brain functions via microchips (or even without them, according to the latest technology) to computers via satellites in the U.S. or Israel, poses the gravest threat to humanity. The latest supercomputers are powerful enough to monitor the whole world's population. What will happen when people are tempted by false premises to allow microchips into their bodies? One lure will be a microchip identity card. Compulsory legislation has even been secretly proposed in the U.S. to criminalize removal of an ID implant.

Are we ready for the robotization of mankind and the total elimination of privacy, including freedom of thought? How many of us would want to cede our entire life, including our most secret thoughts, to Big Brother? Yet the technology exists to create a totalitarian New World Order. Covert neurological communication systems are in place to counteract independent thinking and to control social and political activity on behalf of self-serving private and military interests.

When our brain functions are already connected to supercomputers by means of radio implants and microchips, it will be too late for protest. This threat can be defeated only by educating the public, using available literature on biotelemetry and information exchanged at international congresses.

115

One reason this technology has remained a state secret is the widespread prestige of the Psychiatric Diagnostic Statistical Manual IV produced by the U.S. American Psychiatric Association (APA) and printed in 18 languages. Psychiatrists working for U.S. intelligence agencies no doubt participated in writing and revising this manual. This psychiatric "bible" covers up the secret development of MC technologies by labeling some of their effects as symptoms of paranoid schizophrenia.

Victims of mind control experimentation are thus routinely diagnosed, automatically as mentally ill by doctors who learned the DSM "symptom" list in medical school. Physicians have not been schooled that patients may be telling the truth when they report being targeted against their will or being used as guinea pigs for electronic, chemical and bacteriological forms of psychological warfare.

POWER OF THE MILITARY-INDUSTRIAL COMPLEX

Jan Wiesemann has written an apt description of the situation that now exists in the United States, about the 'forces that be' and how the situation came about:

"During the Cold War the United States not only engaged in a relatively open nuclear arms race with the Soviet Union, but also engaged in a secret race developing unconventional mind control weapons. As the intelligence agencies (which prior to the Second World War had merely played a supporting role within the government) continued to increase their power, so did the funds spent on developing techniques designed to outsmart each other.

"And as the U.S. intelligence community began to grow, a secret culture sprang about which enabled the intelligence players to implement the various developed techniques to cleverly circumvent the democratic processes and institutions...

"Like many other democracies, the U.S. Government is made up of two basic parts the elected constituency, i.e., the various governors, judges, congressmen and the President; and the unelected bureaucracies, as represented by the numerous federal agencies.

"In a well-balanced and correctly functioning democracy, the elected part of the government is in charge of its unelected bureaucratic part, giving the people a real voice in the agenda set by their government.

"While a significant part of the U.S. Government no doubt follows this democratic principle, a considerable portion of the U.S. Government operates in complete secrecy and follows its own unaccountable agenda which, unacknowledged, very often is quite different from the public agenda."

The secrecy involved in the development of the electromagnetic mind control technology reflects the tremendous power that is inherent in it. To put it bluntly, whoever controls this technology can control the minds of everyone.

There is evidence that the U.S. Government has plans to extend the range of this technology to envelop all peoples, all countries. This can be accomplished, is being accomplished, by using the HAARP Project for overseas areas and the GWEN network now in place in the U.S.

116

Dr. Michael Persinger, Professor of Psychology and Neuroscience at Laurentian University, Ontario, Canada, has discovered through intensive research that strong electromagnetic fields can affect a person's brain.

"Temporal lobe stimulation," he says, "can evoke the feeling of a presence, disorientation, and perceptual irregularities. It can activate images stored in the subject's memory, including nightmares and monsters that are normally suppressed."

Dr. Persinger wrote an article a few years ago, titled: *On the Possibility of Directly Accessing Every Human Brain by Electromagnetic Induction of Fundamental Algorithms*. The abstract reads:

"Contemporary neuroscience suggests the existence of fundamental algorithms by which all sensory transduction is translated into an intrinsic, brain-specific code. Direct stimulation of these codes within the human temporal or limbic cortices by applied electromagnetic patterns may require energy levels which are within the range of both geomagnetic activity and contemporary communication networks. A process which is coupled to the narrow band of brain temperature could allow all normal human brains to be. affected by a sub-harmonic whose frequency range at about 10 Hz would only vary by 0.1 Hz."

"Within the last two decades a potential has emerged which was improbable, but which is now marginally feasible. This potential is the technical capability to influence directly the major portion of the approximately six billion brains of the human species, without mediation through classical sensory modalities, by generating neural information within a physical medium within which all members of the species are immersed.

"The historical emergences of such possibilities, which have ranged from gunpowder to atomic fission, have resulted in major changes in the social evolution that occurred inordinately quickly after the implementation. Reduction of the risk of the inappropriate application of these technologies requires the continued and open discussion of their realistic feasibility and implications within the scientific and public domain."

INFLUENCE FROM ABOVE: MIND CONTROL SATELLITES

Unknown to most of the world, satellites can perform astonishing and often menacing feats. This should come as no surprise when one reflects on the massive effort poured into satellite technology since the 1957 launch of the Soviet satellite Sputnik caused panic in the U.S. A spy satellite can monitor a person's every movement, even when the "target" is indoors or deep in the interior of a building or traveling rapidly down the highway in a car, in any kind of weather (cloudy, rainy, stormy). There is no place to hide on the face of the earth.

It takes just three satellites to blanket the world with detection capacity. Besides tracking a person's every action and relaying the data to a computer screen on earth, amazing powers of satellites include reading a person's mind, monitoring conversations, manipulating electronic instruments and physically assaulting someone with a laser beam. Remote reading of someone's mind through satellite technology is quite bizarre, yet it is being done; it is a reality.

It is difficult to estimate just how many people world wide are being watched by satellites, but if there are 200 working surveillance satellites (a common number in the literature), and if each satellite can monitor 20 human targets, then as many as 4000 people may be under satellite surveillance. However, the capability of a satellite for multiple-target monitoring is even harder to estimate than the number of satellites; it may be connected to the number of transponders on each satellite, the transponder being a key device for both receiving and transmitting information.

A society in the grips of the National Security State is necessarily kept in the dark about such things. Obviously, though, if one satellite can monitor simultaneously 40 or 80 human targets, then the number of possible victims of satellite surveillance would be doubled or quadrupled. As early as 1981, G. Harry Stine (in his book Confrontation in Space), could write that Computers have read human minds by means of deciphering the outputs of electroencephalographs (EEGs). Early work in this area was reported by the Defense Advanced Research Projects Agency (DARPA) in 1978. EEG's are now known to be crude sensors of neural activity in the human brain, depending as they do upon induced electrical currents in the skin.

In 1992, *Newsweek* reported that "with powerful new devices that peer through the skull and see the brain at work, neuroscientists seek the wellsprings of thoughts and emotions, the genesis of intelligence and language. They hope, in short, to read your mind." In 1994, a scientist noted that "current imaging techniques can depict physiological events in the brain which accompany sensory perception and motor activity, as well as cognition and speech."

In order to give a satellite mind-reading capability, it only remains to put some type of EEG-like-device on a satellite and link it with a computer that has a data bank of brain-mapping research. I believe that surveillance satellites began reading minds—or rather, began allowing the minds of targets to be read—sometime in the early 1990s. Some satellites in fact can read a person's mind from space.

A surveillance satellite, in addition, can detect human speech. Burrows observed that satellites can "even eavesdrop on conversations taking place deep within the walls of the Kremlin." Walls, ceilings, and floors are no barrier to the monitoring of conversation from space. Even if you were in a high-rise building with ten stories above you and ten stories below, a satellite's audio surveillance of your speech would still be unhampered. Inside or outside, in any weather, anywhere on earth, at any time of day, a satellite in a geosynchronous orbit can detect the speech of a human target. Apparently, as with reconnaissance in general, only by taking cover deep within the bowels of a lead-shielding fortified building could you escape audio monitoring by a satellite.

There are various other satellite powers, such as manipulating electronic instruments and appliances like alarms, electronic watches and clocks, a television, radio, smoke detector and the electrical system of an automobile. For example, the digital alarm on a watch, tiny though it is, can be set off by a satellite from hundreds of miles up in space. As well, the light bulb of a lamp can be burned out with the burst of a laser from a satellite.

In addition, streetlights and porch lights can be turned on and off at will by someone at the controls of a satellite, the means being an electromagnetic beam which reverses the light's polarity. On the other hand, a lamp can be made to burn out in a burst of blue light when the switch is flicked. As with other satellite powers, it makes no difference if the light is under a roof or a ton of concrete – it can still be manipulated by a satellite laser. Types of satellite lasers include the free-electron laser, the x-ray laser, the neutral-particle-beam laser, the chemical- oxygen-iodine laser and the mid-infra-red advanced chemical laser.

Along with mind reading, one of the most bizarre uses of a satellite is the ability to physically assault someone. An electronic satellite beam—using far less energy than needed to blast nuclear missiles in flight – can "slap" or bludgeon someone on earth. A satellite beam can also be locked onto a human target, with the victim being unable to evade the menace by running around or driving around, and can cause harm through application of pressure on, for example, one's head. How severe a beating can be administered from space is a matter of conjecture, but if the ability to actually murder someone this way has not yet been worked out, there can be no doubt that it will soon become a reality. There is no mention in satellite literature of a murder having been committed through the agency of a satellite, but the very possibility should make the world take note.

There is yet another macabre power possessed by some satellites: manipulating a person's mind with an audio subliminal "message" (a sound too low for the ear to consciously detect but which affects the unconscious). In trying thereby to get a person to do what you want him to do, it does not matter if the target is asleep or awake. A message could be used to compel a person to say something you would like him to say, in a manner so spontaneous that no one would be able to realize the words were contrived by someone else; there is no limit to the range of ideas an unsuspecting person can be made to voice.

The human target might be compelled to use an obscenity, or persons around the target might be compelled to say things that insult the target. A sleeping person, on the other hand, is more vulnerable and can be made to do something, rather than merely say something. An action compelled by an audio subliminal message could be to roll off the bed and fall onto the floor, or to get up and walk around in a trance. However, the sleeping person can only be made to engage in such an action for only a minute or so, it seems, since he usually wakes up by then and the spell wears.

It should be noted here that although the hypnotism of a psychoanalyst is bogus, unconscious or subconscious manipulation of behavior is genuine. But the brevity of a subliminal spell effected by a satellite might be overcome by more research. "The psychiatric community," reported Newsweek in 1994, "generally agrees that subliminal perception exists; a smaller fringe group believes it can be used to change the psyche."

A Russian doctor, Igor Smirnov, whom the magazine labeled a "subliminal Dr. Strangelove," is one scientist studying the possibilities: "Using electroencephalographs, he measures brain waves, then uses computers to create a map of the subconscious and various human impulses, such as anger or the sex Dr.ive. Then, through taped subliminal messages, he claims to physically alter that landscape with the power of suggestion."

In the August 22, 1994 issue of Newsweek, Dr. Smirnov revealed that the FBI asked advice from Smirnov during the siege at Waco. Smirnov said "The FBI wanted to 'pipe subliminal messages from sect member's families through the telephone lines into the compound."

SPECIAL BONUS SECTION

For David Koresh the group's leader... the FBI had in mind a special voice: "God as played by the famous actor Charlton Heston."

In this case, the sect members would be influenced by electromagnetic high frequency voices of their relatives, and David Koresh would hear in his head the voice of God played by Charlton Heston. Smirnov told the FBI that they would have to find the individual frequencies of the sect members if the idea was to work correctly.

Combining this research with satellite technology – which has already been done in part – could give its masters the possibility for the perfect crime, since satellites operate with perfect discretion, perfect concealment. In many countries the military operates tracking stations; assisting the giant American National Security Agency. The NSA covertly monitors every call, fax, e-mail, telex and computer data message. The relevant computers search for key words/phrases. Anything/anyone of interest is drawn to the attention of agency operatives. This can lead to a large-scale personal surveillance operation by the NSA or other agencies; like the CIA and their criminal connections. The current system is called ECHELON.

The magnetic field around the head is scanned as you are satellite tracked. The results are then fed back to the relevant computers. Monitors then use the information to conduct a conversation where audible neurophone input is applied to the victim.

The neurophone was developed by Dr. Patrick Flanagan in 1958. It's a device that converts sound to electrical impulses. In its original form electrodes were placed on the skin but with defense department developments, the signals can be delivered via satellite. They then travel the nervous system directly to the brain (bypassing normal hearing mechanisms). Dr. Flanagan's 3D holographic sound system can place sounds in any location as perceived by the targeted/ tortured listener. This allows for a variety of deceptions for gullible victims.

Today, various top-secret groups use satellites and ground based equipment to deliver verbal threats, deafening noise and propaganda; using neurophone technology. Anything from TV's/radio's appearing to operate when switched off through to "Voices from God" and encounters with aliens are all cons using neurophone technologies to torment, deceive and (most importantly) discredit agency/criminal targets. Naturally, the system can mimic anyone's voice and automatic computer translations (into any language) are incorporated.

Human thought operates at 5,000 bits/sec but satellites and various forms of biotelemetry can deliver those thoughts to supercomputers located worldwide that have a speed of 20 BILLION bits/sec. These, even today, monitor thousands of people simultaneously. Eventually they will monitor almost everyone.

Usually the targets are aware their brain waves are being monitored because of the accompanying neurophone feedback. In other words, the computer repeats (echoes) your own thoughts and then the human monitors comment or respond verbally. Both are facilitated by the neurophone.

There is little time left to make the rest of the world aware of the nefarious operations now in effect. Our rights and freedoms as human beings are in jeopardy if these warnings continue to go unheeded.

**BEFORE HER UNTIMELY DEATH, A CONTROVERSIAL ABDUCTEE
DECLARED THAT THE EVIDENCE WAS IN . . .**

MORE FOE THAN FRIEND -- IS IT TIME WE FORM
AN ALIEN RESISTANCE?
By Sean Casteel

For many in the UFO community who deeply desire a more reassuring explanation for the UFO phenomenon than the evidence may present, Karla Turner continues to be a problematic, even tragic figure in the many years since her death in 1996 from a dangerous form of breast cancer she contracted right after an abduction experience. Turner was an outspoken voice for abductees' rights and never wavered in her belief that the aliens were an evil, invasive force that intended no good with their medical experiments and frightening mind control capabilities. To this well-educated, gifted woman, the UFOnauts were wickedness personified, simply evil in the "flesh."

The publisher, *"The Conspiracy Reader,"* is adamantly determined that Karla Turner's voice continues to be heard from beyond this time and place and that her message is still proclaimed in an era when alien abduction is no less rampant and no less traumatic for the experiencers than when Turner first began writing about what was happening to her and her family. This is more so the case considering that so many stand deeply-rooted today in the Exopolitical movement, where a sort of pseudo-hip "spiritual blissfulness" regarding the true character of the "visitors" outweighs rational thought in light of what at least some of the evidence as to their nature seems to indicate. This can no doubt be considered a "theme book" which utilizes not only Turner's searingly painful research, but added background material from a stable of writers, which includes Timothy Green Beckley, Tim R. Swartz, Brad and Sherry Steiger and myself, resulting in a rather hefty, large format, 285-page collection of shocking, mind-warping accusations against those who seemingly hold us in some form of cosmic slavery that has gone on unabated possibly since antiquity if not from the start of our very existence here.

This innovative book, "Evil Empire of the ETs and the Ultra-Terrestrials," opens with a fascinating narrative by seasoned UFO/paranormal author Tim Beckley, who first hung out his journalistic shingle in the field over forty years ago. In a section which he justifiably titles "Strange Brew," Beckley – who has long heralded the paranormal vs interplanetary genesis for the UFO enigma – relates the harrowing tale of a succession of tormented travelers who encountered strangely morphing ships and shape-shifting beings while driving the open highway, turning their sojourns into hellish nightmares. In one case, a married couple, Bob and Jackie Blair, told their story to a newspaper reporter in Sauk Centre, Minnesota.

"They had been experiencing unexplainable phenomena for three days," the newspaper states, "for 900 miles across three states, and when they stopped in Sauk Centre, Minnesota, hardly anyone believed them."

The pursuit had begun in Montana when what the Blairs at first took to be stars in the night sky turned out to be nine small ships and one large one. Things turned hostile quickly when the couple's car was shot with needle-like shavings of silver metal that penetrated the couple's windshield. The shavings ruined the truck's new paint job and when Jackie touched them they caused her fingers to break out in blisters; Bob had a similar blister on his wrist. The reporter says that their fingers glowed from the unknown substance they had touched and Bob exclaimed, "We might be dying right now! We don't know what it is. We have to get to a doctor."

The incident is dead on creepy as the couple says that a group of attacking "individual things" were "shaped like about eight-inch people with V-shaped heads, wings on their backs," like prehistoric birds. They were said to be exceedingly hostile and went into attack mode several times, cloaking the scene in a dense fog. "It was like a backwards tornado coming from the mouth of the leader of the ships. It was like a ray that he was sending down with this funnel. He did it five times, than left," Bob said.

This is a classic example of the kind of mental and emotional agony often left behind after a UFO encounter.

"And you know we're not dealing with men from Mars," says Beckley, who was once a strong believer in the interplanetary origins of the UFO phenomenon but has wavered from this path in recent years. Not knowing or understanding what has happened is hard to bear, especially in a case where one is forced to wonder whether some kind of life-threatening injury has been incurred. How could Bob know whether the blisters he and his wife had were somehow a sign of something fatal? What doctor could have treated an alien-induced sickness?

Beckley's chapter provides the entire eye-popping scenario of the Blairs along with another terrifying highway encounter that happened to a young woman named Mickie and her girlfriend, which is so blatantly bizarre that it would appear that they were almost on an acid trip, though Beckley says they swore to him in a face to face interrogation that they never touched the stuff. At one point in their drive across country a monster "dog" appeared in their back seat complete with glowing red eyes, scaring the bejesus out of the two women. Beckley believes this adds considerable weight to the Ultra-Terrestrial concept that other realities are merging with our own in many close encounter cases, placing the abnormalities outside the realm of wandering spaceships and alien occupants into a totally different conceptual dimension

My own contribution is called "The Shadowy Universe of Alien Thought Control," and deals with such unsettling possibilities as the mental co-opting of world leaders in government, religion and economics and the open hostility of the alien presence. In an interview I did with researcher and political activist Michael Brownlee, he argues quite convincingly that if anyone else were to abduct members of our citizenry by the millions or over-fly and disable our nuclear missile sites, we would regard it as an act of war and respond accordingly.

Why is it we give the aliens a free pass in those terms? One answer may be that we are humiliatingly outgunned and outmanned, and the authorities simply can't go public with a situation they can neither influence nor control. However, efforts like the Star Wars Space

Defense program, begun under President Ronald Reagan, seem to be a step in the right direction, Brownlee said, and he knows personally people in the defense industry who are continuing to work to develop adequate technology to fight back against the aliens' superior weaponry.

There is also new material in "Evil Empire of the ETs and the Ultra-Terrestrials" by veteran authors Brad and Sherry Steiger, whose chapter is called, simply enough, "Hostile Encounters With Alien Intelligences." One can always count on the Steigers to produce some of the very best writing on this subject available anywhere, and their chapter certainly no exception.

"The Not-So-Friendly Face Of ET Encounters" is offered here by writer and Emmy Award-winning producer Tim R. Swartz, who never fails to deliver an in-depth and thorough examination of the topics he writes about.

Sandwiched in between all the fascinating new material is of course Karla Turner's "Into The Fringe," which set new standards for honesty and bravery in the face of the dark mystery of alien abduction. Turner had no patience for people who said the negative baggage that accompanies abduction was because of the abductee's failure to be open to the experience's beauty and worth. Like Brownlee, she protests most vigorously the tendency to "blame the victim," to say the fault lies in humanity and not in the fascistic, iron-grip of the aliens. No amount of New Age positive thinking can change the fact that people are being subjected, completely involuntarily, to a series of medical, psychological and emotional procedures that leave them cowering in fear and with no readily available cure or solution.

Even the late Budd Hopkins, who told me more than once that he hesitated to call the aliens "evil" because it would an over-simplification that he felt would be counterproductive, nevertheless equated alien abduction with rape, simply because it was not an experience freely chosen and could not be stopped by any human method of resistance.

For an article she wrote for Tim Beckley's now defunct magazine "UFO Universe," which is further elaborated on in the recent Global Communications book "Round Trip To Hell In A Flying Saucer," Karla Turner created a checklist, a breakdown of the most basic elements of alien abduction that puts the matter in its proper perspective quite succinctly. We present a portion of the checklist here.

- Aliens can alter our perception of our surroundings.
- Aliens can control what we think we see. They can appear to us in any number of guises and shapes.
- Aliens can take us – our consciousness – out of our physical bodies, disable our control of our bodies, install one of their own entities, and use our bodies as vehicles for their own activities before returning our consciousness to our bodies.
- Aliens can be present with us in an invisible state and can make themselves only partially visible.

- A surprising number of abductees suffer from serious illnesses they didn't have before their encounters. These have led to surgery, debilitation, and even death from causes the doctors can't identify.

- Some abductees experience a degeneration of their mental, social and spiritual well-being. Excessive behavior frequently erupts, such as drug abuse, alcoholism, overeating and promiscuity. Strange obsessions develop and cause the disruption of normal life and the destruction of personal relationships.

- Some abductees report being taken to underground facilities where they see grotesque hybrid creatures, nurseries of hybrid humanoid fetuses, and vats of colored liquid filled parts of human bodies.

- Abductees report seeing other humans in these facilities being drained of blood, being mutilated, flayed, and dismembered, and being stacked, lifeless, like cords of wood. Some abductees have been threatened that they, too, will end up in this condition if they don't cooperate with their alien captors.

- Aliens have forced their human abductees to have sexual intercourse with aliens and even with other abductees while groups of aliens observe these performances. In such encounters, the aliens have sometimes disguised themselves in order to gain the cooperation of the abductee, appearing in such forms as Jesus, the Pope, certain celebrities, and even the dead spouse of the abductee.

"It becomes clear," Turner writes, "from these details that the beings who are doing such things can't be seen as spiritually enlightened, with the best interests of the human race in mind. Something else is going on, something far more painful and frightening, in many, many abduction encounters."

There is an understandable need, she acknowledges, for humans to believe in the power of good.

"We need for the aliens to be a good force," she admits, "since we feel so helpless in their presence. And we need for some superior force to offer us a hope of salvation, both personally and globally, when we consider the sorry state of the world."

The aliens understand that we hope for them to be benevolent creatures, she reasons, and they use that desire for goodness to manipulate us.

"What better way to gain our cooperation," Turner asked, "than to tell us that the things they are doing are for our own good? Looking at the actions, the results of alien interference, such as on the list above, there is a great discrepancy between what we desire from them and what they are doing to us."

Turner also detailed the consistent patterns of deception that make up a great deal of the abduction experience. People sometimes report that they were treated kindly by the aliens, and were told that they were "special" or "chosen" to perform some important task for the benefit of humanity. Given such a positive message, the abductees may ignore the fear and pain of their encounters and insist to themselves and others that a higher motive underlies the abduction experience. They may only recall, in some cases, a benevolent encounter and have no memory of any negative action.

But intensive research now shows us something much different.

"We know, for instance," Turner writes, "that 'screen memories' are often used to mask an alien abduction. Such accounts abound, in which a person sees a familiar yet out-of-place animal, like a deer or owl, a monkey or a rabbit, and then experiences a period of missing time. The person often awakens later to find a new, unexplained scar on his body.

"Uneasiness about the encounter will persist, however, and far different memories may start to surface in dreams or flashbacks, and then the person seeks help to explain the uneasiness. Quite often, hypnotic regression is used to uncover the events behind the 'screen memory,' and that is when the typical alien abduction surfaces. However, from several recent cases, it is apparent that these recovered memories may well be yet another screen, masking events that are much more reprehensible."

So, according to Turner, abductees can't trust their screen memories nor can they trust the recovered memories which may come later. It quickly becomes a wickedly complex hall of mirrors in which the truth perishes somewhere in the many reflected surfaces. If things like forcible sexual intercourse and all the other forms of victimization can be defended in moral terms, we are a long way from understanding how.

Turner's voice was not the only one shouting to be heard with this unhappy truth, and many abduction researchers and hypno-therapists agree with her overall negative take on the experience, though they may not express it in those same exact terms. Ann Druffel, for instance, has written extensively about methods for resisting alien abduction, one of which involves invoking the name of Jesus immediately after an experience begins.

But it is Turner who remains the most eloquent spokesperson for resistance from among the abductees, and we can only wonder if her voice was silenced by her death from cancer as a deliberate act of the aliens, who were intent on enforcing some form of damage control to counter the "bad press" she was giving them. Such a thing is unknowable of course; the vagaries of when an illness like cancer presents itself may have nothing to do with aliens, even in Turner's case.

Nevertheless, reading "Evil Empire of the ETs and the Ultra-Terrestrials" will help to keep Turner's dissenting voice alive and perhaps aid in your own coming to terms with experiences that continue to bewilder and frighten you. If you have a difficult time making it all fit into a rosy, glowing picture, you are certainly not alone.

The great bard Shakespeare once famously wrote, "The fault, dear Brutus, is not in our stars, but in ourselves." But perhaps, in the case of alien abduction, the fault originates somewhere out there in the stars after all.

[If you enjoyed this article, visit Sean Casteel's "UFO Journalist" website at www.seancasteel.com to read more of his work and to purchase his books.]

The Not-So-Friendly Face of ET Encounters
By Tim R. Swartz

The galaxy is teaming with planets. In fact, it appears that there are more planets than suns in the Milky Way. Most astronomers now suggest that with so many planets, it is almost a certainty that intelligent life must exist somewhere in the vast cosmos. If there are intelligent creatures on other worlds, what can we expect of them? Would they be friendly or hostile?

Zhu Jin, director of the Beijing Planetarium, asserts that aliens wouldn't harm earthlings if they do pay us a visit someday.

"Extraterrestrial civilizations most likely exist. Personally, I don't think they would hurt earthlings because they have to travel countless light-years to get to here. The feat itself indicates that their civilization has developed to such a degree that violence has become almost impossible."

Many scientists agree that a civilization capable of interplanetary travel has evolved beyond the primitive emotions that create violent tendencies. As well, if these same scientists went to the trouble to examine the UFO phenomenon, they would conclude that whoever is piloting the UFOs must be friendly, or at least indifferent to the inhabitants of planet Earth.

However, a more detailed analysis of the interactions between humans, UFOs and the creatures associated with them, reveal a completely different, and very disturbing conclusion altogether.

ANGELS FROM OUTER SPACE

Starting in the early 1950s, men such as George Adamski and Howard Menger claimed that they were in contact with benevolent extraterrestrials who allegedly were the pilots of the mysterious flying saucers. The so-called "Space Brothers" were almost indistinguishable from humans, and claimed to be visiting Earth because of their concern for the destructive spiritual path that humanity was taking. The UFOnauts wanted to save us from our war-like ways and guide us towards a galactic utopia shared by practically all intelligent interplanetary races.

For all intent and purposes, the Space Brothers were angels in physical form, preaching a new gospel of cosmic enlightenment and brotherhood. All humanity had to do was to stop fighting each other, dismantle our atomic weapons, and we would be welcomed into the loving arms of our brothers and sisters from outer space.

When you take into consideration the era, the whole concept of friendly, if not almost nurturing, aliens from outer space is surprising. The 1950s was a time of extreme mistrust and almost pathological paranoia. Both the United States and the Soviet Union were determined to eliminate each other at any cost, and this atmosphere of hatred spilled over into almost every aspect of life. Cold War paranoia was especially evident in popular culture such as movies and television.

1950s science fiction movies such as *War of the Worlds, Invasion of the Body Snatchers, and Earth vs. the Flying Saucers* popularized the notion that aliens from other planets had only one motive, to take over and destroy the Earth. You would think that the UFO phenomenon would have reflected popular culture. However, the alleged "real" contacts with space aliens were just the opposite from their mass-media counterparts.

Was this always the case, or did the "less-than-friendly" UFO encounters get swept under the rug by those who were advocating the "Happy Space Brothers" scenario?

Visitors from Beyond Time and Space

Unidentified flying objects have been zipping through the skies of planet Earth as long as there have been people around to watch them. Ancient writings, folklore and religious texts are full of tales of unusual, glowing airships and the weird creatures contained within them, and much like the UFOs, the strange beings inside come in an amazing and prolific range of extraordinary shapes and sizes.

For someone whose only knowledge of UFOs comes from the popular media, this may seem perplexing. After all, anyone who has watched television or gone to the movies in the last twenty years knows flying saucers are spaceships carrying little gray men from outer space. The gray alien with large black eyes has seemingly supplanted the hundreds of other weird beings reported over the last sixty years by UFO witnesses. However, the gray alien stereotype is a relatively recent addition to the pantheon of "aliens" that have interacted with mankind throughout history.

What is strange is the almost complete disappearance of the friendly Space Brothers, replaced by the less-than-friendly grays. The Space Brothers interplanetary lectures on the path of universal spirituality had been replaced by frightening middle of the night abductions and painful surgical procedures.

Since the late 1970s, the abduction experience has captured the majority of attention in the field of UFO research. Much has been written about how to the abductees, these experiences seem to be purposely generating as much pain and fear as was possible. This seems to be an almost 360 degree turn around from the earlier reports of UFO occupants inviting witnesses onboard for tea and cookies and a quick tour around the solar system. It's not as if in the past the only interactions with UFO occupants were pleasant and harmonious. There were numerous cases all over the world where a UFO sighting ended up being an extremely dangerous experience.

According to the website *Weird Australia*, during 1951 in the Gungal district of the Hunter Valley, NSW, prospector Graem Stout, was told by local Aboriginals that a "huge saucer" airship had descended upon six Aborigines setting up their campfire beside a local creek to cook their evening meal. Apparently, the UFO "sucked them all up through a big hole underneath it" then flew away with them. The six Aborigines had vanished from the face of the Earth.

In 1953, a lone bushwalker in the rugged Burragorang Valley in the Blue Mountains spotted a group of "man-like figures wearing shiny white "space suit-like outfits".

Watching them from behind some bushes, the humanoids appeared to be "searching the ground with strange metallic devices, apparently collecting soil samples". This all sounds innocent enough, however soon after this event occurred, three young bushwalkers went missing in the same area…and according to researcher Rex Gilroy, were never located.

Beware the Little People

In 1979, researchers from MUFON's Humanoid Study Group compiled a long list of more than 1,600 different UFO entity incidents. Contrary to the popular belief that sightings of UFO beings are generally rare, researchers found that many of the reports are well-documented, firsthand investigations involving credible witnesses.

The most frequently reported of all the UFO occupant cases are dwarf-like creatures that average three to four feet in height. Their complexion ranged from dark and swarthy to very pale, often bordering on white, although reddish and bluish skin colors have also been mentioned. One of the more bizarre groups of UFO creatures seen, especially in the 1950's, was the animal-like hairy dwarves.

In the early morning hours of November 28, 1954 two truck drivers from Caracas, Venezuela, Jose Ponce, and Gustavo Gonzales were driving to Petare, about fifteen miles away from Caracas. Around 2:00AM, the men found their way blocked by a glowing disc-shaped object about ten feet in diameter, which was hovering about six feet above the street.

Gonzales brought his truck to a stop and both men got out and walked closer to the object. When they were about twenty-five feet from it, they discovered they were being approached by what appeared to be a very hairy dwarf-like man.

Gonzales impulsively grabbed the creature and lifted him off the ground, but the creature twisted out of the truck driver's grasp and gave Gonzales a shove that sent him sprawling backward.

Before Gonzales could regain his feet, the humanoid, whose eyes glowed in the headlights of the truck like yellow cats' eyes, leaped on the man and began to claw at him with webbed hands that had claws about an inch long. Gonzales later told police that he tried to fight back with a knife into the creature's shoulder . . . but the blade glanced off of the creatures shoulder as if it were made of steel. At this point Jose Ponce panicked and ran to seek help from a nearby police station.

As Gonzales tried to fight off his strange attacker, another hairy little man jumped out of the glowing craft and pointed a small shiny tube at the man. There was a brilliant beam of light that briefly blinded Gonzales. When he could see again, the object was rising above the trees and quickly shot away.

Gonzales ran for the police station and showed up a couple of minutes after Ponce. At first police thought the men were drunk or crazy. A doctor determined that both men were in a state of shock and that neither of them had been drinking. Gonzales was treated for a long deep scratch down his left side and later reports said that it eventually healed but left a permanent scar.

A few weeks later, on the night of December 16, 1954, three young men were driving on the outskirts of San Carlos, Venezuela, after a night out on the town. Jesus Paz asked his friends to stop the car so that he could relieve himself. Paz walked about 12 feet away from the parked car when he suddenly screamed and dropped down into the tall grass. His friends ran to his rescue and found him stunned and lying on the ground. A short distance away, a small, hairy, manlike creature was running toward a shiny disc-like craft that was resting on the ground. The hairy dwarf disappeared inside of the object which quickly rose off the ground with a loud buzzing sound and vanished into the night sky.

Paz was rushed back to the city to the hospital, where doctors found that he was in a state of shock. Furthermore, the man had long deep scratches on his right side and downward across his spine "like claw marks" the doctor said.

Paz told officials that he had walked around a bed of tall flowers when he almost stumbled over a short, hairy manlike creature that was examining the flowers. Paz tried to escape, but when he turned, the creature attacked him with its long talons, clawing and tearing his shirt, and striking Paz on the back of the neck.

Several weeks later, Paz told a local reporter that his scratches had still not healed properly, remaining red and inflamed as the day when he was injured. After his initial interview, Paz refused to discuss his encounter ever again.

They Might Be Giants

On the opposite end of the scale are the UFO giants. Even though their reports are not nearly as numerous as the small humanoids, the UFO giants certainly are the most bizarre of the UFO occupants.

The giants are the least humanlike of all reported entities - with sightings describing creatures seven to nine feet tall and an amazing diversity ranging from one-eyed Cyclops, beings with black-faces, bushy black hair, and in some instances, with three unblinking eyes and large, round heads.

One amazing giant story was the account of a truck driver named Eugenio Douglas who allegedly used a revolver to fight off three "shiny metal robots" some fifteen to twenty feet tall. This happened in Argentina on October 18, 1963.

Douglas told police that he drove his truck into a ditch after a brilliant white light engulfed it near the town of Monte Maix. The light, he said, came from a twenty-five-foot disk parked in the middle of the road.

When he got out of his truck, three "indescribable beings" approached Douglas and tried to grab him. He managed to draw his pistol and fire several shots at the giants, who seemed unfazed by the bullets. Nevertheless, Douglas managed to get away and run toward town as the saucer lifted off the road and made several passes at him. He said that each time he felt "a wave of terrible, suffocating heat." The police examiner later found that Douglas had suffered several unusual burns, unlike anything he had seen before.

What is Going On?

It is clear that we have no idea what is really going on with the UFO phenomenon. Good...evil...or both? Perhaps trying to place such human terms as Good and Evil to the situation is like saying a tornado that destroyed a town is evil. Such concepts simply do not apply to UFOs and the forces behind them.

Books such as Brad Steiger's "*Flying Saucers Are Hostile*" and Harold Wilkins "*Flying Saucers On The Attack*" prove at least some of the UFOs are seemingly out to get humans. Steiger mentions an entire African village was destroyed by a beam of light projected from a UFO. Jerome Clark in his article "Why UFOs are Hostile" mentions the possibility of "hundreds, possibly thousands" of people being murdered around the world by UFOs."

Referring to Steiger's book, Clark says UFOs or their occupants have been responsible for aggravated assault, burnings by direct ray focus, radiation sickness, murders, abductions, pursuits of cars, assaults on homes, paralysis, cremations, disrupting power sources, etc. Clark says there is also "no objective evidence apart from contactee cases, that UFOs are friendly or from other planets."

The book, "*UFOs: What on Earth is Happening*" (1976, Bantam Books, by John Weldon with Zola Levitt) does an excellent job of listing why UFOs and their occupants are not something to be sought out.

"There are also dangerous physical effects resulting from close association with UFO beings or craft. These include blackouts, blindness, sexual assault, psychological disturbances, painful skin infections, chronic headaches, convulsive seizures and even cancer. In the case of those who claim personal contact with extraterrestrials (contactees), they have reported being programmed, deceived and made to look like fools. They have experienced the loss of jobs and experienced family disruptions. Reportedly, there are frequent cases of insanity, particularly paranoid schizophrenia, found among contactees and at times, they are commanded to murder others... There are a very large number of sudden or mysterious deaths, suicides and nervous breakdowns among UFO investigators."

A close examination of close encounters with UFO occupants indicates that the occupants seem to be habitual liars. They often contradict each other and espouse obviously false beliefs. The UFO pilots have said that their homes are Mars, Venus, Saturn, Jupiter, a hidden world behind the sun, the hollow Earth and various other places throughout the galaxy. Many of these strange reports receive little attention because they do not fall within the boundaries that UFO researchers have imposed on what they consider acceptable cases.

The incredible variety of UFO occupants should give serious researchers' pause to reconsider the popular theory that UFOs are interplanetary spaceships. For unless planet Earth is some sort of intergalactic truck stop, it is difficult to explain why each UFO occupant sighting tends to be unique. However, whatever their origins or purposes, one thing is clear, UFOs can be dangerous and the best course of action is to not seek them out, and to stay as far away from them as possible.

Are Black-Eyed Beings Walking Among Us?
By Ted Twietmeyer

This is perhaps one of the strangest topics that scores about a 20 + on the weirdness scale of 1 to 10. First, we should take a brief look at some of the characteristics of the human eye as to what's normal and what isn't. The white part of a human eye is called the sclera, which comprises 5/6 of the outer surface of the eye. The sclera is a very thin tissue made of several layers, with a total thickness varying between .3mm and 1mm thick depending on where on the eye it's measured.

I should mention here for reference later that human eyes are filled with a clear, gelatinous material known as the vitreous humor. This material must be crystal-clear to permit the unobstructed passage of light from the rear of the lens to the retina. Some people have "floaters" in their eyes, which are minerals or crystals and may cause strange glints of light when in a brightly lit area.

Regardless of race, most healthy humans have a white color (or nearly white) sclera. Other life-forms such as horses, dogs, lizards etc often have a dark brown or black sclera.

BLACK-EYED BEINGS

Are there beings or people among us whose sclera, pupils and iris are completely BLACK? We will refer to them as beings, because at this time we really don't know who or what they are. There are numerous eye witness accounts of people like this in almost every location you can imagine, and from many corners of the Earth. We will look at some of those accounts later.

Below are some common characteristics of black-eyed beings I've discovered from examining eyewitness testimony:

* Sometimes the adult or child dresses in attire to fit into the local population, but odd variations can also cause the black-eyed person to stand out. Eyewitness accounts have stated that the clothing is either overly neat as though they are from a by-gone era, or have strange color combinations.

* Black-eyed beings may dress in black or dark clothes

* When black-eyed children approach adults they do not act shy like normal children. Instead, they are often quite forceful about what they want from the adult and may try to intimidate or persuade. These children may be verbally forceful in demanding entry into a home or a vehicle on a public street, but apparently they do not become physical.

* Evil is a common characteristic that eyewitnesses often sense from both black-eyed children and adult beings. However, this feeling is not experienced by every eyewitness.

* In public places such as restaurants or airport gate waiting areas, often people will not sit anywhere near them especially after making eye contact.

* It is possible that some (or all) of these beings do not have a home, and are roaming the Earth endlessly. One eyewitness who was alone with a man in an elevator late at night asked him where he was going. His curt response was "NOWHERE!"

* These beings have been reported by people world-wide, and are not known to originate from any particular location on Earth.

* One eyewitness was in an elevator with a black-eyed being. The following day he checked a security camera videotape but it did not record the presence of the black-eyed being in the elevator. Only the eyewitness was seen alone on the videotape.

* A common occurrence among children with black eyes is to ask permission to enter a vehicle or a home. Apparently there are certain laws these beings must follow, such as being invited in. What's interesting is that this law requiring permission is known to apply to supernatural evil, such as demons. If laws ruling supernatural interference did not exist, then all of humankind would be in utter chaos and terror, and society could never develop to the level of what it is today.

* Solid form - unlike ghosts or other disembodied entities, eyewitness accounts have not spoken of transparency. These black- eyed beings appear to be solid and can speak verbally, although this does not negate a supernatural origin.

* Some accounts indicate that at least some of these beings have olive colored skin.

* Eyewitness accounts of these beings often take place at night or inside buildings. Perhaps they cannot tolerate direct sunlight.

* Black-eyed adults could be related to the "Men in black" (MIB) who have also appeared with pitch black eyes to intimidate UFO witnesses. MIB often appeared to those who make it past a close encounter of the first kind. There haven't been any new accounts of MIB visits in recent years that I know of. Perhaps these black- eyed beings are of the same race as the MIB, who may now be unemployed.

Many years ago we had a relative who was an albino (now deceased.) An albino is the result of a genetic mutation that prevents pigment generation anywhere in the body. Her skin was extremely light, almost white but slightly pink as a result of no pigmentation to fully cover the fine blood vessels. Her hair was always white even when she was quite young. The sclera of her eyes was basically devoid of all white color, resulting in a pinkish-red color from the coloring of blood vessels in the thin sclera. However, she did not normally wear glasses as her vision was close to normal. This is mentioned here to show that human beings who are albino would be at the far opposite end of the spectrum from black-eyed beings.

In black-eyed beings, apparently the sclera is black as well as the pupil and iris. Witnesses are probably not seeing the retina directly. Humans have the classic red-eye in photographs as a result of flash photography. To see into the eye of a black-eyed being would probably require a similar intense on-axis light source. However, if eyewitnesses can actually see a black retina as some have claimed, then the retina of these beings must absorb light even better than the eyes of human beings.

Late at night in the headlights of an oncoming vehicle on a highway deer, opossums and other animals have eyes (retinas) have a green or red color. This is a retro-reflection from the animal's retina. It is similar to how a reflector on a bicycle or driveway marker reflector works. Human beings have a non-reflective retina, reflecting back only about 1% of the light that enters the eye.

One might dismiss these strange black-eyed people as a rare genetic mutation, except for one simple fact that apparently no one talks about - If both the sclera is black AND the vitreous humor inside the eye is black as well, these beings would almost certainly have to be blind since no light could reach the retina through black vitreous humor.

EYEWITNESS ACCOUNTS

Below are some relevant excerpts from several very lengthy eyewitness accounts.

(A note here to the grammar nit-pickers: There are grammatical, typographical errors and other problems in these accounts, but these statement extracts have been retained as the eyewitness has written them to avoid changing any intended meaning. I have added a few statements in parentheses for clarity. If I've made errors myself in this essay, forget about it!)

AT HOME LATE ONE NIGHT

A lady named Adele was at home when two boys knocked on her door at 11PM at night. What follows is a verbatim excerpt from her testimony. After a long introduction Adele began to describe the boy's details:

"He was young boy of about 17 or 18, approximately," Tee says. "He asked me about an open apartment for rent. I remember feeling very scared and shaken by his appearance. He did not look weird by his dress or such. It was his eyes. I remember feeling the hair on my neck stand up, and I was shaking just from looking in his eyes."

Like Chris, Tee also felt that deep sense of malevolence. "I could not look him straight in the eyes," she says. "I felt like I was about to die. Now, some people may think that I was just over- reacting or something, but the eyes were completely black - like there was no real pupil. He spoke normally to me, but I had to just shut the door in his face and get as far from him as I could. I felt like I was in extreme danger." [2]

(What might have happened to Adele if these children were allowed entry into her home?)

MAN SITTING IN A CAR ON A STREET

In this incident which took place in Abilene, Texas, a journalist was in his parked car late at night writing a check to pay an internet bill at a drop box when two children approached him for help, knocking on his car window. They were asking for a ride home to retrieve money from their mother to see a popular movie, at the movie theater close to the parked vehicle. What made this event highly unusual to the witness was that these children asked for a ride home when the final showing of the film was already half over. The following is a verbatim excerpt from his account. One of the two boys is identified as the "the spokesman" by the eyewitness. He is the only boy who talked during the discussion. When the eyewitness was reluctant to let the boys into his car they persisted. Here are his words:

"C'mon, mister. Let us in. We can't get in your car until you do, you know," the spokesman said soothingly.

(Note the child was apparently following the unspoken law that permission must be granted first as indicated by the statement "We can't get in your car until you do, you know." The testimony continues)

"Just let us in, and we'll be gone before you know it. We'll go to our mother's house." We locked eyes. To my horror, I realized my hand had strayed toward the door lock (which was engaged) and was in the process of opening it. I pulled it away, probably a bit too violently. But it did force me to look away from the children. I turned back. "Er ... Um ...," I offered weakly and then my mind snapped into sharp focus.

For the first time I noticed their eyes. They were coal black. No pupil. No iris. Just two staring orbs reflecting the red and white light of the marquee. At that point, I know my expression betrayed me. The silent one had a look of horror on his face in a combination that seemed to indicate: A) The impossible had just happened and we've been found out!" The spokesman, on the other hand, wore a mask of anger. His eyes glittered brightly in the half-light. "Cmon, mister," he said. "We won't hurt you. You have to LET US IN. We don't have a gun."

That last statement scared the living hell out of me, because at that point by his tone he was plainly saying, "We don't NEED a gun." He noticed my hand shooting down toward the gear shift. The spokesman's final words contained an anger that was complete and whole, and yet contained in some respects a tone of panic:

"WE CAN'T COME IN UNLESS YOU TELL US IT'S OKAY. LET ... US .... IN!"

I ripped the car into reverse (thank goodness no one was coming up behind me) and tore out of the parking lot.

(Question is - do these boys actually have a home? What might have happened to the eyewitness IF they were allowed entry into his vehicle?)

AIRLINE PASSENGER

In another work-for-word account a black-eyed man boarded a commercial airliner. Apparently some sort of mind control was being used, as flight attendants and the captain all saw different colors in this same man's eyes, including pitch black:

I glanced up just in time to see a late arriving passenger, noting his well-appointed leather jacket, pants and shoes all were nice complimentary shades of brown. His haircut was in the European cut with tendrils on the nape, instead of the precise American haircut. I froze as I looked into his eyes. They were black in entirety. He looked European or a light Arabian. I don't remember seeing the white part of his eyes.

(Flight attendant continues) That man is very scary, I am so afraid. I was very frightened too, ready to pee my pants. I laid my arm on the door ledge and watch out the porthole and wondered if we would survive this trip. The feeling was unanimous with the other girls and we were on total edge. I was pondering why each of us thought his eyes were a different color.

(Later in the flight she describes the man's eyes) We were so distressed that the Captain put on his hat to come out for a look. That passenger closed his eyes and appeared to be sleeping. We landed without ado and matter of fact, the airplane emptied in world record time about 2-3-minutes. This man was coming and the Captain was saying goodbye. I refused and hopped back into the galley. I whispered, "Here he comes and I watched the Captain as all the color drained from his face, when the man passed out the door. The captain said, WOW...whoa that was a strange man!

(If this black-eyed man was not human, how did he obtain a boarding pass?)

BANK BUILDING IN AUSTRALIA

Here is another verbatim extract from a story about a strange man seen in an elevator in a bank building, as told by the bank executive who worked late that evening:

I found to my surprise that a few people have had similar experiences regarding people with pitch-black eyes. Unlike some, though, I didn't feel a sense of dread or a feeling that I was about to die. I felt more an awareness and discomfort, like when you see someone advance angrily toward you only to walk past you.

Anyway, it was September 2, 2000, and one of the roles as an executive is you sometimes have to put in really late nights. My office was on the fifth floor and it was coming up to 12 in the morning. I was the only employee, as far as I know, on the first five floors apart from Ben, another fellow banker on my floor and Stan, who is a security officer.

(He continues after a lengthy introduction) The elevator stops at floor 2 and in comes a tall man with more or less a black crew-cut. The first thing I did was open my mouth to ask what sector he was from and who gave him permission, but as I looked into his eyes they where entirely black. The pupils, the retinas everything. I remember not really being spooked about his eyes. To be honest, I just thought he might've had a disability in his eyes. As the elevator slowly starts up moving back on route, he asked me where I was going, and I simply replied, "home." He then asked why, and I more or less laughed and just said I want to go to sleep and see my wife. He then just mummered very softly, like he was talking to himself, "It must be nice to have a home."

I figured he was just being friendly and that he must be renting. As we got to B1, I realized he hadn't pushed the button on where he was going, so I asked, "Where are you going?" to which he replied rather angrily looking at me with his creepy eyes, "Nowhere."

(At this point, the eyewitness stated he ran to his car. When he looked behind him, he noticed the strange man in the elevator did not get out. He continues on with his account)

Now the real freaky part. As I drove down the street, all the lights were out - and this is in Sydney (city of NSW). Then I turn... and guess who is walking just ahead of the car - our favorite black-eyed man! No need to say, I sped home, probably breaking five road laws. How could he have left the building and be ahead of me when he had no car, and went up to floor 6?

It gets weirder. On the videotapes and records, there shows no one using the elevator at that time apart from me.

BLACK-EYED BEING IN STARBUCKS

Witness begins her statement that it was a nice sunny day in November and she had been out running some errands. No country, state or city is given but it may have be in the United States. Although it was November, the black-eye being wore no coat or jacket. Perhaps this took place in the southern United States:

I got my tea, headed out the door, had to stop and organize myself as my keys migrated to the bottom of the purse and I still had to get my wallet in! So I plopped the stuff down on an open table and tried to get my act together. I felt like I was being watched, so turned around to give whatever to the perv that I assumed was watching me, and the smart aleck remark died in my mouth as I caught sight of him and made (inadvertent) eye contact.

I should note here: I did not see anything unusual in his manner of dress. Jeans, black shirt, lightweight black jacket, (no hat, no overcoat) not unusual dress. His hair was almost black, but didn't look any darker than my boyfriend's hair (boyfriend is of Japanese descent). His skin tone was a bit olive and pale but not overly so. It was the eyes and the aura, coming off of him that scared me.

The eyes, blacker than black, no white at all, wall to wall black, and I just felt a darkness around him, an evil. As I looked in his eyes, I somehow KNEW that was not a human soul occupying that body, and I felt that he knew that I knew that he was not human.

Interesting side note: three open tables around the table "he" was sitting at, were empty, and stayed empty. People would just come out the door, look in that direction, and leave. No one would sit near "him".

I got the feeling that "he" was amused by this. That he could keep humanity away and he was challenging me, "Are you going to run away too?" My reply was "I am leaving because I was planning on leaving." (All this was telepathic.)

BLACK-EYED WOMAN SEEN IN MICHIGAN

A woman and her husband stopped at their usual rest stop in Michigan on the way to their second home for a short vacation. Below is an excerpt from her account:

My husband and I were on our way up north on I-75 during the afternoon. Luckily, it was not at our normal time in the evening. We have a little place in northern lower Michigan, and often go up there for the weekends. As was our custom, we pulled in at our usual rest stop, and I went into the women's restroom.

As I was preparing to leave the room, I suddenly noticed a thin, dark-haired woman standing alone and starring directly at me. I instantly felt a terrible sense of dread, as though there was something deeply unnatural about her. I then noticed the eyes which had been staring coldly at me, and they were completely black. I saw no color whatsoever, and no pupils. I felt an extremely strong need to get away from her as quickly as possible, as there was something quietly threatening about her. Her stare was devoid of any emotion other than something very cold and disconnected.

My instant and unwavering feeling during this whole experience was that she was not human. I don't know what me made feel this so strongly, but it was my most singular, strongest sense while looking at her. There also was something almost predatory about her, as though she was homing in on prey while she stood there so still. I also had a strange sense of her feeling superior or stronger in some way. Again, the sense of a predator watching its prey.

I left as quickly as possible, showing as little reaction to her as possible. It seemed important, for some unknown reason, for me to act unaffected by her while in her presence. I felt a huge sense of relief as I got back into the car and left. I have to say that this was one of the most memorable brief experiences I've ever had around a person, especially a stranger. I have never been able to shake the unexplainable feeling that she wasn't human.

BLACK-EYED CHILD SEEN AT YMCA IN CALIFORNIA

Here is yet another verbatim extract from a sighting in Encinitas, California:

(After her introduction she continues) I work at the local YMCA as a youth counselor, one night as I sat in the parking lot clearing room on the seat next to me for my friend to sit down this kid comes up to the side of the car, immediately as this kid gets near us we can tell something is wrong, my friend just hopped into the back of the car and we lock all the doors. The kid didn't say anything, but before I realized it I had rolled down the window, when I got a closer look at the kid I was alarmed at how young he looked, I'd say about 7-10 years old.

He was your average very blonde white kid, pale skin, but he gave off a terrible aura of bad things. He told me to let him in the car, never giving a reason, I was compelled by some force to open the door, but my friend kept telling me "there's no more room" The kid began to repeat this phrase back, sounding very angry. "NO MORE ROOM, NO MORE ROOM" at this point he and I made eye contact, I saw that his eyes were fully black, no whites to them at all. He grabbed my arm through the window, and dug his fingernails into my forearm, his skin was cold. I shoved him from the window and shouted "THERE'S NO MORE ROOM" and slammed my foot on the accelerator. We drove over the curb and flattened a bush before leaving the parking lot, as we sped towards my friend's house we saw this kid twice, once at a fruit stand, and again at a red light.

(Two days later another black-eyed child appears outside the eyewitness's home)

We go back to watching the movie when there is a knock on the door. Not just one or two, but a knock that you get when someone is angry with you, like when the government comes in all the movies. I look out the peephole and see no one, so I opened the door. Standing there is a teenage kid, pale skin, jet black hair. I ask him if he needs help, and he told me he needed a telephone. This kid looks fairly straight-edge, he looks like the type you can trust, I get no bad aura from him, and I'm about to let him in when I notice his eyes. Deep black, just like the kid in the parking lot. I slam the door in his face, and look out the peephole, I still see no one through it. [3]

Are all of these eyewitness accounts fiction?

This seems unlikely as those who wrote them were not seeking fame or fortune, so what could possibly be a motive to fabricate these stories? Most likely, there are thousands or tens of thousands of these sightings but most people haven't taken the time to document them, or know where they can be posted.

There are common characteristics to each of these eyewitness accounts of something that often triggers a human innate sense of evil, fear, night time appearances, a certain peculiar forcefulness and sometimes a sense of terror of the unknown.

Perhaps these black-eyed beings are one of the 63 races visiting Earth (this was the last total known according to a retired Air Force officer friend of mine.) Or maybe these beings have the ability to come and go from another dimension that co-exists with ours, which is hopefully not hell.

If these black-eyed beings are not human but are inter-dimensional, alien or of supernatural origin it might explain why they do not appear on a video recording in at least one case. Yet these beings are real, physically exist and communicate with people according to eyewitness accounts.

Herman Melville once said, "The eye is the gateway to the soul." If the eye of these beings really is completely black, then this might be an ominous message about who these beings are.

[1] https://tspace.library.utoronto.ca/bitstream/1807/5513/1/ dv05060.pdf
[2] http://paranormal.about.com/od/humanenigmas/a/aa090406.htm
[3] http://www.freewebs.com/thekingofwolves/index.htm

Write for our free catalog:

Global Communications
P.O. Box 753
New Brunswick, NJ 08903

Email: mrufo8@hotmail.com

www.conspiracyjournal.com